Games (and More!) for Backpackers

Drawings by
WENDY WALLIN

GAMES (AND MORE!) FOR BACKPACKERS

JUNE FLEMING

A PERIGEE BOOK

Perigee Books
are published by
The Putnam Publishing Group
200 Madison Avenue
New York, New York 10016

Copyright © 1979 by June Fleming
All rights reserved. This book, or parts thereof,
may not be reproduced in any form without permission.
Published simultaneously in Canada by General Publishing
Co. Limited, Toronto.
Published by arrangement with the author

Library of Congress Cataloging in Publication Data

Fleming, June.
   Games (and more!) for backpackers.

   Reprint. Originally published: Portland, Or. :
Victoria House, c1979.
   "A Perigee book."
   Bibliography: p.
   1. Games for campers.   I. Title.
GV1202.C36F57   1983   794   82-21432
ISBN 0-399-50712-4

First Perigee printing, 1983
Printed in the United States of America
1 2 3 4 5 6 7 8 9 10

To Collin and Brynn,
with thanks for sharing many wilderness celebrations
. . . beginning with the pie pans and Three-Fingered Jack

Also by June Fleming

The Well-Fed Backpacker

The Outdoor Idea Book

CONTENTS

Introduction   15

SECTION I: MAKE-AT-HOME PROJECTS   17-41

Puzzles, *with instructions for making and solving*
- String and Bead Puzzle   18
- Nail Puzzle   19
- Block Puzzle   20
- Contour Puzzle   21
- Buttonholer   22
- The Hexer   23
- Tangram   24

Boomerang, *collapsible for packing,*   24-25

Coordination Toys
- Paddle and Ball   26
- Paddle Golf   27
- Pin and Balls   27-28
- Rings and Stick   28
- Cup and Ball   29

Two Old Folk Toys
- Buzz Saw   29
- Mountain Bolo   30

Six-Sided Stumpers, *letter cubes for many word games*   31

Put and Take   32

Game Board, *small and versatile*   32
    with instructions for
- Fox and Geese   33
- Solitaire   33
- Migration   33

Nature Discovery Tools
- Plant Press   34
- Waterscope   35

Music   36-40
- Wood Harmonica   36
- One-String Dulcimer   36-37
- Cross Flute   38
- Finger Cymbals   38-39
- Matchbox Harp   39
- Strawhorn   39-40
- Comb-and-Paper Kazoo   40
- Mouthbow   40

SECTION II: IN THE FIELD   43-93

Tuning in to the Wilds   45-61
    Lists as You Walk   45
    Walk Silently   45
    Listen   45
    In-Depth Discovery of Camping Area   45
    Nature Scavenger Hunt   46
    Wildlife Observation at Night   46
    The Rock Recognition Game   46
    Intensive Survey   47
    Collect Feathers   47
    Collect Scats   47
    Animal Track Casts   47-48
    Study Aquatic Life   48
    Animal Track Sketches   48
    Attract Birds   49
    Make a Poem: Haiku, Cinquain   49
    Plant, Bird, and Mammal Lists   49-50
        of all you know   49
        plants with animal names   49
        birds named for . . .   49
        mammals named for . . .   50
    Stargazing, some helpful tools   50
    Predicting the Sun's Path   50-51
    Find North without a Compass   51
    How Much Daylight Is Left?   51-52
    Expand Your Map-Reading Skills   52

    Get Friendly with Your Compass   53 - 55
        Parts of the Compass   53
        Orienting   53
        Taking a Bearing   53
        Following a Bearing   54
        Finding Your Way Back   54
        Exercises for Practice   54-55

    Bolstering Your Botanical Vocabulary   58-61
        Six Favorite Flowers   58
        Common Shrubs and Trees   58
        Think Scientific Names   58
        Story Game   58
        Botanical Dictionary   59-61

    Mind and Mouth Games (*no special equipment needed*)   62-67
        Endless Chain   62
        Twenty Questions   62
        Word Pairs   62
        Name Stretch   62-63
        Granny's Backpack   63
        Sing Out   63
        Watt Zynonym?   64
        Sentenced   64
        Cartographer's Delight   64
        Hig-Pig   65
        Tongue Tanglers   65
        What Am I?   66

Lists Galore 67
I'm Thinking of . . . 67
Boil This Down 67

Games That Need a Little Equipment 68-77
   Word Grid 68
   Keep Your Eyes Peeled 69
   Points for Pairs 69
   Derivation 70
   Quick Change 70
   One Minute of Words 70
   Profiles 70
   Expansion 70-71
   Weave-a-Word 71
   Triangle Capture 71
   Number Tic Tac Toe 71-72
   Whimsical Word Weaving 72
   Story Ball 72
   Teamwork Tales 72
   Two-Sided Dice 72-73
   Match Games 73-74
   The Sandwich Game 74
   Dara 75
   Nine Men's Morris 75
   Puzzles for Fingers and Minds 76-77
      Cube Sides 76
      Dimes and Quarters 76
      Reversing the Pyramid 76
      The Volga Boatman 76
      Coded Circle 76
      Magic Fifteen 76
      Five-Vowel Words 76
      Multiplying Amoeba 77
      Stick Puzzles 77
      Puzzle Answers 94-95

Card Games 78-80
   Albanian Dwarfs 78
   Spoons 78-79
   Speed 79
   Twitch 80

Body and Senses Games 81-88
   Juggling 81
   Grass-Blowing Ensemble 81
   Sleeping Giant 81
   Blowing Bubbles 81
   Whittling 81
   Penny Pitch 81
   Kite-Flying 82
   Collect for a Wall Hanging 82
   Ooooh-Aaaah 83
   Hone Your Senses 83
   Hand Shadows 84-85
   Make Some Music 86-87
      Instruments 86
      Play Your Nose 86

    Name That Tune   86
    Dueling Harmonicas   86
    Spoons   87
    Detective   88
    Wilderness Charades   88

Tie One On . . . Knot Games   89

String Figures   90-93

SECTION III: CATALOG OF PACKABLE PLEASURES   97-109

From Toy Stores, Department Stores, and Stationery Stores   98-99
    Old Favorites   98
    Pocket Games   98
    Pocket Puzzles   98
    Paper and pencil games   98
    Word games   98-99
    Card games with special decks   99
    Action toys   99
    Telescopes, hand magnifying lenses   99
    Musical instruments   99

From Art Supply Outlets   100

From Music Stores: *things to blow, slide, tootle, tap, clack, hum, strum and twang*   101-102

Music by Mail: *instruments and kits*   103

Mail-Order Games   103

Flying Things: *kites and boomerang*   104

Nature Tools: *Audubon bird call, sunprint kit*   104

Books   105

Items for Viewing Tiny or Faraway Objects   106-107

Suppliers' addresses   108-109

Games (and More!) for Backpackers

GAME HARDWARE

When a game in the wilderness calls for **playing pieces,** many things will work fine:

- coins
- buttons
- checkers
- poker chips
- pebbles
- beans
- rice grains
- cone scales
- sunflower seeds
- nuts
- raisins
- candies
- matchsticks
- bits of paper
- golf tees (trim off ½ inch to save bulk)
- sliced dowel (an old broomstick makes checker-sized pieces, and smaller dowels also serve well)

If you need a **playing board** with squares marked off:
- ◻ Make a one-time board by drawing lines on paper.
- ◻ Use your hiking map with its built-in grid lines.
- ◻ Lay out a grid on the ground with string, straight twigs or lines scratched in the dirt.
- ◻ Take a more durable cardboard grid from home.
- ◻ Make a lasting board from a piece of wood 4 inches square and ½ inch thick.
- ◻ To make shallow holes that will hold marbles or small rocks, use a large bit.
- ◻ For peg holes, drill small holes deep enough to hold matchsticks or golf tees, but not all the way through the board.
- ◻ A dual-purpose portable playing board can be worn on your head! Cut and hem a 16-inch square scarf from lightweight fabric any light, solid color. With a dark laundry marker or indelible felt-tipped pen, mark off a 2-inch grid, 8 boxes square. Crosshatch alternating squares to represent the black ones on a checkerboard.

INTRODUCTION

Most of the time, wilderness adventures provide their own fun and relaxation — it's built-in. But often there's a need or opportunity for extra recreation, and most of us have given some thought to the shapes it can take. Stormbound hours in a tent need filling, the warmth of friendship warrants a celebrative game, and trail-weary bodies want less vigorous activity.

Ideas in this book could rescue spirits on a trip when the weather turns rotten. Instead of getting bored, restless and grumpy stuck inside your tent, you can be stretching your mind, testing your wits and happily enjoying a new game with friends. And when the elements are kind, there are still plenty of relaxing hours when an outing is enriched by some group fun and less strenuous pastimes than the day's trail-walking.

This book was born when several of us were en-tented during a spring snowstorm in Oregon's Cascades. After a few rounds of cribbage and playing Hawaiian tunes on our noses, Dave reached into his pack and produced "Oscar's Toy," a simple but fun and challenging coordination toy, a variant of the age-old ring-and-pin game. We all agreed there must be dozens of similarly totable amusements that would make hikers' off-hours very pleasant. So I began researching game lore, toys and musical instruments to find things that could be adapted to packing and wilderness use. The field is vast, since play has been around as long as people, always an integral part of man's existence. Packable play abounds, with something for virtually every taste.

From these numerous possibilities, I chose many activities that can bring pleasure to the lone traveler, a whole raft of two-person pastimes, and other games for small groups. I include diversions that represent many points along the play scale from "serious, edifying, think-hard" to "frivolous, silly, pointless but jolly fun." So the person who doesn't consider himself the party-games sort should be able to find just as many appealing ideas here as one who gets a kick out of lighthearted frolicking.

There are plenty of mind games and word games to delight the cerebral part of you. There are puzzles to challenge your perseverance, sense of order, reasoning, and recognition of spatial relationships. Some of the games depend largely on luck, so they're fun for those who aren't as quick of reflex or as skilled as their fellow players. Others call forth all the clever turns of mind you can manage.

Throughout the book I tried to weave a thread that would connect readers to the wilderness environment. Sometimes this thread is simply an outdoor version of a standard game, with the side benefit of encouraging recall of the names of places or growing things. Other lengths of the thread are specially designed environmental games that are definite learning experiences, either increasing some skills (such as wildlife observation, map reading, knot tying), honing the senses, or nudging folks into intensive explorations of the wilderness setting.

This book is divided into three basic sections:
1. things to make at home
2. in-the-field pleasures that require little or no advance preparation
3. a catalog of packable pleasures you can buy, both in retail stores and mail-order outlets

I believe it's possible to have fun in the wilds without abusing them. Therefore, I tried to include in this book activities that:
- have minimal impact on the environment
- are fun, relaxing, challenging
- bring out your playful spirit
- are imaginative and spur your creativity
- can be used in various ways (I make some suggestions and hope you'll be inspired to invent new ways to use a basic structure or play word games)
- use little or no equipment (if required, it is compact, lightweight, fairly sturdy, and can often be made cheaply, easily, quickly)
- can be done alone or with just one or a few friends (no team games for groups of 12; my conviction is that more than 8 voices and 16 feet concentrated in one area are too many)
- increase your wilderness skills, knowledge, caring, and desire to know it intimately
- are suitable for a wide age range but chiefly appeal to adults with lots of the child in them

You *won't* find activities that:
- are hard on the land, such as run-around games that could disturb the ground and its cover, games that require cutting/collecting/changing more than a small amount of materials present in the natural-state environment
- have a consistent, necessary high noise level and can't be done any other way
- need a large, flat, stable surface
- require lots of complex, bulky, heavy and/or expensive equipment

In all your wilderness fun, *please* leave the place the way you find it, or *better*. Think twice when you're tempted to romp in a lovely clearing, home to countless plants and crawling and burrowing creatures, and dinner table for many browsers. Damage is easily done and slowly repaired. Make judicious use of noisy games and music, limiting them to situations where you won't offend nearby seekers of quiet.

This book is designed to be toted along on your wilderness adventures as well as used at home while planning and preparing for outdoor fun. It will easily slip into a small space in your pack and is durable enough to be *used*! I hope it will earn a place on your basic checklist for a backpack trip.

Section I:
MAKE-AT-HOME PROJECTS

Here are twenty-eight projects to prepare ahead of your wilderness trips: games, puzzles, toys, musical instruments, and items to help you explore and study the outdoors. Some take just a few minutes' time and cost pennies; others are more complex and cost a little more. All are happy additions to your backpacking gear and will give many years of pleasure.

STRING AND BEAD PUZZLE

The object is to move the bead from one loop to the other.

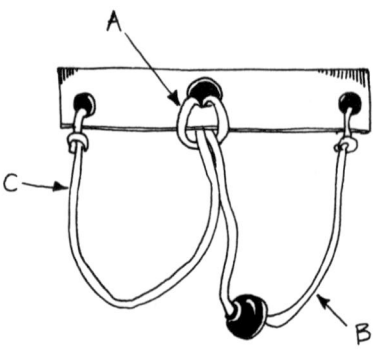

TO MAKE

1. Cut a piece of cardboard (or thin wood, for a more durable version) about 4 inches by ¾ inch.
2. With a paper punch (or drill), make a small hole near each end and a larger hole in the center.
3. Attach an 18-inch piece of sturdy string with a bead threaded as shown. Be sure the bead is larger than the center hole and the string substantial enough to withstand a lot of manipulation while folks figure this one out.

TO SOLVE

1. Pull down loop A and move the bead along string B until it is inside loop A.
2. Reach behind the puzzle and pull the two strings coming out of the center hole so that loops B and C are pulled through the center hole to the back.
3. Slide the bead along its string through the loops made by B and C on the back side of the puzzle.
4. Now from the front side, pull loop A forward through the center hole, bringing strings B and C with it.
5. The bead is now on string C. Slide it down through loop A, and the puzzle is solved!

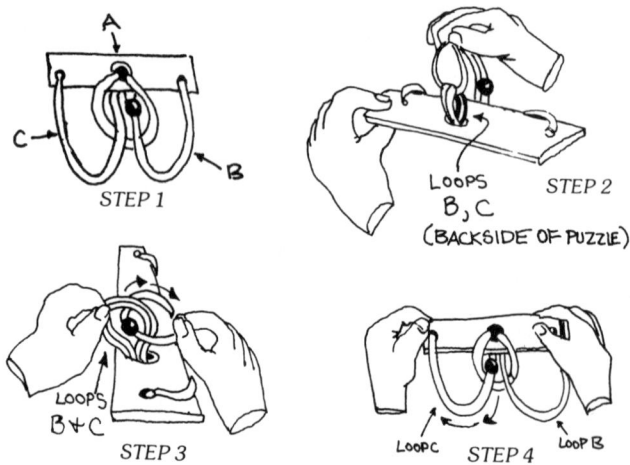

NAIL PUZZLE

Like the string and bead puzzle, this one has a long history of challenging and baffling people. It is simply made and simply worked, once you figure out the procedure; but just when you think you've mastered it, the solution may elude you.

TO MAKE

Start with two skinny nails 4 to 6 inches long, and bend each into a 270-degree twist, as shown. This is done by hammering each nail around a ½-inch pipe (clamp nail and pipe in vise). The gap in each bent nail must be too small to allow the other to pass through.

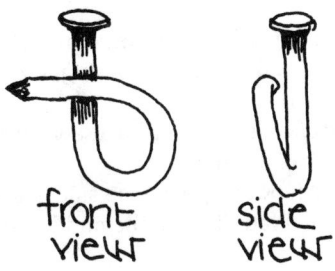

TO SOLVE

The goal is to separate, then rejoin, the two nails. Hold one steady in your left hand and work the other through the positions shown with your right hand until the nails come apart easily. Go backwards through the steps to put the puzzle back together.

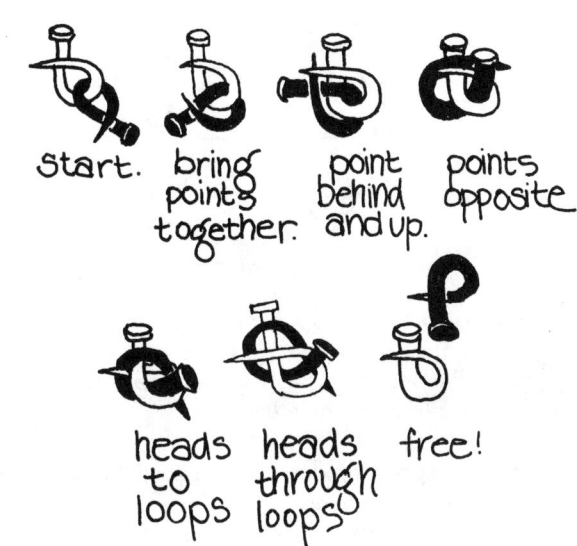

BLOCK PUZZLE

It is said that this six-piece wooden puzzle was designed in Japan many years ago as an exercise in cabinetry, with the challenge of having the pieces join snugly. However, even a rank amateur in the workshop can turn out a serviceable model. A little rattle doesn't stand in the way of fitting the puzzle together.

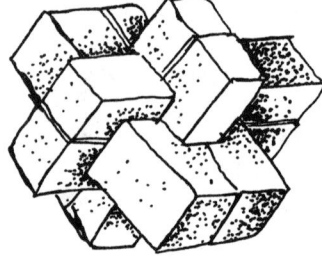

TO MAKE

1. Start with a piece of 1 x 1, 21 inches long. Cut it into six pieces, each 3½ inches long.
2. Sand all rough ends. Set aside one piece, which becomes piece A; it's complete as is.
3. Make three piece B's:
    a. On two opposite sides, draw a pencil line lengthwise down the middle of the piece.
    b. On an unmarked side, draw two lines across the piece, 1 inch in from the ends. With a coping saw, make a cut on these lines halfway through the piece (that is, to the lengthwise pencil line).

c. Now remove this section with a small chisel or carving tool, working from the side with a lengthwise line.
4. Make two piece C's, which are the most complicated.
    a. On all four sides of the pieces, draw lengthwise pencil lines down the middle.

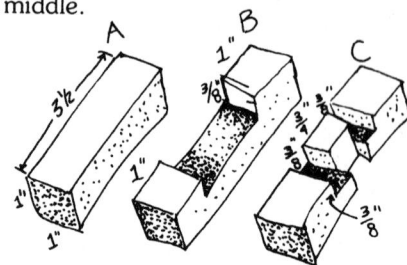

b. On all sides, draw lines across the piece, 1 inch in from the ends.
c. Draw vertical lines that subdivide the middle section on all four sides into three parts, measuring 3/8 inch, 3/4 inch and 3/8 inch.
d. On one side of each piece make a saw cut on the two inner lines to a depth of 3/8 inch.
e. Turn the piece toward you so the side you just sawed is down. Saw along the four lines of the middle section to a depth of 3/8 inch.
f. Turn the piece away from you and, from the top, carve out the two outer sections of the partly sawed middle section. To do this, place the blade of your tool on the lengthwise dividing line and carefully cut out the two 3/8-inch portions to the right and left of the 3/4-inch section.

g. Turn the piece toward you again and carve away the middle 3/4-inch section along the lengthwise dividing line.

5. Check the pieces for fit, using your carving tool to adjust the cut-out section for a snug fit. Sand rough areas and corners.

TO SOLVE

1. Put two B blocks together on end so their cut-out sections meet.
2. Slide the third B block, cut-out section up, halfway through the opening made by the other B's.
3. Fit the two C blocks horizontally into the cross of the B blocks, as shown.
4. Slide the A block into the center opening, and the puzzle is solved.

CONTOUR PUZZLE

Reassembling this small, sturdy, wooden puzzle will challenge you and your friends. It can be made in varying degrees of difficulty by changing the size of your starting piece of wood and the number of cuts made in it. Carry the assembled puzzle with a rubber band around the middle.

TO MAKE

1. Use a piece of 2 x 4, 5 inches long. From the end, make four random wavy cuts through the 4-inch dimension of the block with a band saw.
2. Make three random wavy cuts through the block on the 2-inch dimension.
3. You now have a three-dimensional puzzle consisting of 20 wavy pieces. If you want a little advantage in assembling the puzzle, separate every other piece in checkerboard fashion and paint half the pieces a color which contrasts with the natural wood.

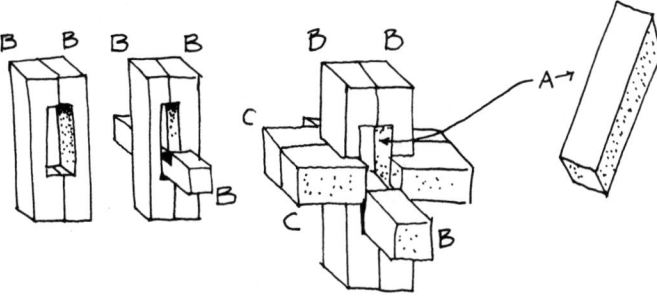
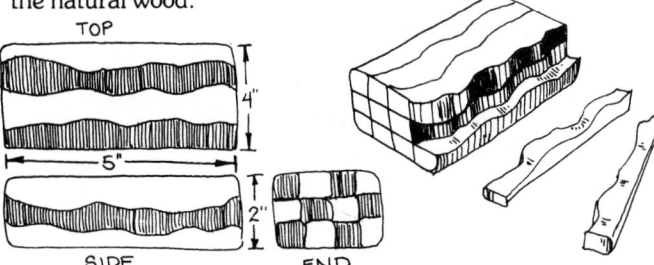

BUTTONHOLER

For the mind that thinks in uncommon ways, this puzzle is good for once around your circle of hiking friends . . . then take it along whenever you're trekking with new folks. The object is to get the string and stick through the buttonhole of a shirt or jacket, as shown, without untying the string.

TO MAKE

1. Drill a small hole at least ¼ inch from the end of a piece of 3/8-inch dowel, 2½ inches long.
2. Put a piece of string through the hole and tie it in a loop that is *too short* for the other end to pass through.

TO SOLVE

The puzzle works best on a shirt or jacket made from fabric that can be wadded up, something not too thick or stiff. A down-filled parka won't do, but a wool shirt is perfect.

1. Bunch up the cloth around the buttonhole, making a small "mountain" of the cloth, with the buttonhole at the top of the mountain.
2. Slip the loop over the buttonhole, down to the base of the mountain, and put the stick through the hole.
3. Smooth out the cloth; the stick is now in place.

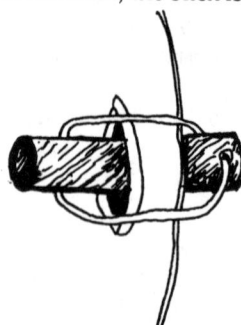

TO UNSOLVE

Bunch up the cloth around the buttonhole, pull the string loop downward and pull the stick out of the buttonhole.

THE HEXER

Puzzles of varying degrees of difficulty can be made from this basic design, all of which fit together to form a hexagon. Our example has six pieces and several possible solutions, but you could use a larger number of pieces and include several not easily distinguished from one another.

TO MAKE

Draw the basic grid according to instructions, then outline the puzzle pieces within it. A 5-inch square of lightweight cardboard works well, but the puzzle can also be made larger or cut from thin plywood.

1. Using a compass, draw a circle with a 5-inch diameter.
2. Draw line AF through the center of the circle.
3. Using the same compass setting and points A and F as centers, draw arcs that intersect the circle at points B and C, D and E.
4. Draw straight lines connecting B and E, C and D.
5. Connect AB, BD, DF, FE, EC, CA.
6. Divide lines AB, BD, DF, FE, EC, and CA in half, marking the divisions with points G, H, I, J, K, L.
7. Draw lines between K and G, J and H, L and H, K and I, I and G, J and L.
8. Your circle is now filled with equilateral triangles. To make the puzzle shown here, combine the triangles into the six shapes shown in the drawing, cut them out and paint the top sides in contrasting colors. For a more challenging puzzle, make more than six pieces.

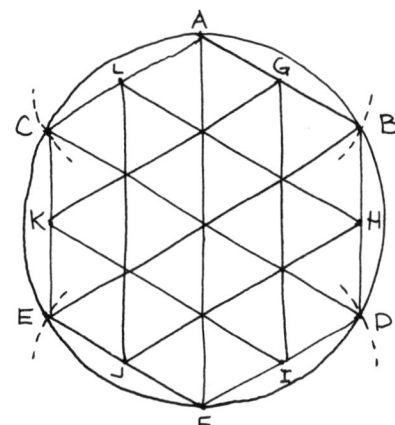

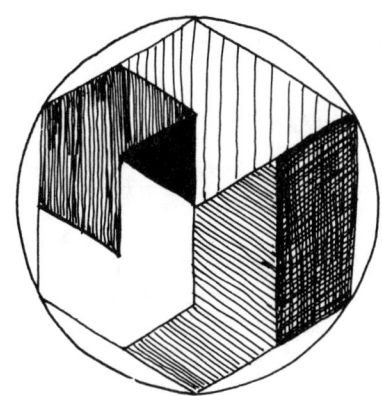

23

TANGRAM

The tangram, of ancient Oriental origin, is a group of seven pieces which can be fitted together to make hundreds of pictures and designs. From a 5-inch square of cardboard (not corrugated), cut the five triangles, one square and one rhomboid according to the diagram. A tangram this size is adequate for playing area about 1 foot square. A more durable puzzle can be cut from thin plywood or a floor tile, but of course it will be heavier.

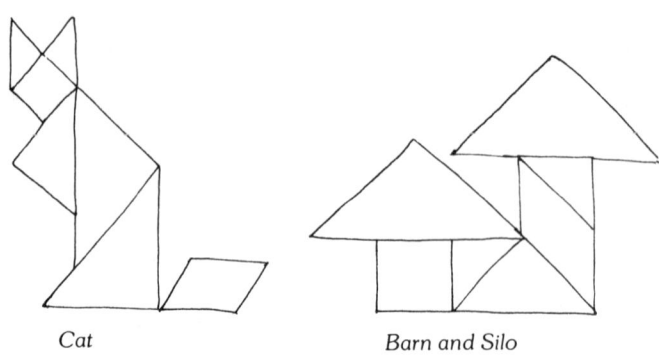

Cat

Barn and Silo

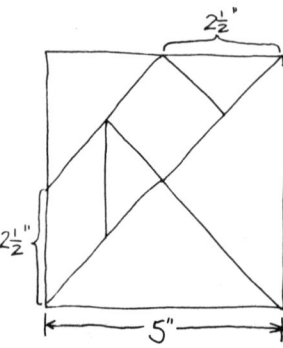

Here are just two of the infinite number of pictures you can make from a tangram. Try making a boat, a fox, a swan, an Indian chief, a flying bird.

BOOMERANG

Did you know that archaelogists have found boomerangs dating back to 10,000 B.C.? That King Tut had one in his tomb? That the Smithsonian Institute has an annual Boomerang Tournament? The art of boomerang throwing has sparked lively interest, and there are dozens of styles and sizes available (see Catalog section, page 99). Called by some ''the thinking man's frisbee,'' today's boomerang is much more than just the traditional modified L used for hunting by primitive peoples.

Your local hobby store carries the basic ingredient for this simple cross-stick boomerang: a 3-foot-long piece of balsa wood 1/8 inch thick and 1 inch wide. Find a bolt (1/8 x 1/2) and wing nut, and spend a few minutes making this collapsible trail toy. The cross-stick style of boomerang is quite accurate and its usual flight path circular, so learning to throw and catch it is a satisfying experience. If there's more than one boomerang in your group, you might want to compete for accuracy in throwing, duration of flight, distance of travel, and number of consecutive catches.

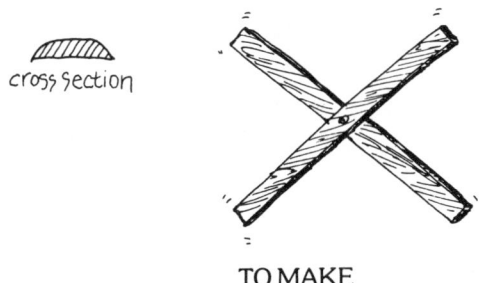

TO MAKE

1. Cut the balsa wood into two pieces, each 18 inches long.
2. Find and mark the center of gravity on each, and mark a 2-inch section in the centers.
3. With coarse sandpaper, bevel the edges on the top sides of the sticks from these lines to the ends. Except for the 2-inch middle sections, the stick is roughly convex in cross-section and the edges uniformly thin. The bottom sides stay flat.

4. Now bend each end of the sticks upward slightly, toward the beveled sides (the tops). To accomplish this, hold the stick over a lighted candle so the flame barely touches the stick 6 inches from the end (be careful not to let it catch on fire!). When heated, grasp the ends of the stick and bend upward slightly, holding the bend for a few seconds. The resulting bend should not be more than ¼ inch.

5. Bolt the two sticks together at right angles, with the curves all in the same direction.

TO FLY

A calm day is most favorable, but if there is a breeze, throw the boomerang directly into it. Since every boomerang flies in its own way, you'll need to experiment a bit to find the best throw for a return. Try tilting it some, putting more or less force into the throw, or aiming your throw at a slightly different angle.

Vertical throw: With your right hand, loosely grip the end of one wing, having the boomerang perpendicular to the ground at eye level, beveled side toward you. Keeping the boomerang perpendicular, draw your arm back and throw it straight forward, snapping your wrist sharply downward just as you release the boomerang.

Horizontal throw: With your right hand, hold the boomerang beveled side up, parallel to the ground, out to your side. Throw it forward and upward, with plenty of spin.

RING AND PIN § PADDLE AND BALL § CUP AND BALL

Dozens of variations of these coordination toys are found in cultures all over the world, and I'll describe just a few here. The aim is always to see how many rings or balls you can catch on a stick, in a cup, or put through a hole. It's harder than it looks, and you'll find your performance is definitely improved by practice. You can raise your skill level quite a bit while waiting out a blizzard!

A **paddle-and-ball** requires:
- ☐ a piece of ¼-inch plywood 6 by 2½ inches
- ☐ one wooden ball 1 inch in diameter
- ☐ heavy string 30 inches long

TO MAKE

1. From the plywood cut a paddle as shown, cutting out a circle 1¼ inches in diameter (drill a starting hole and use a keyhole saw, or use a hole saw with an electric drill).
2. Drill or nail a hole at the large end of the paddle to accommodate the string.
3. Sand the rough edges.
4. Drill a small hole through the center of the ball if it doesn't already have one.

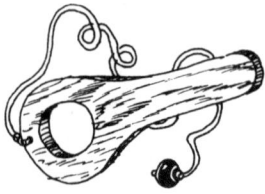

5. Tie a large knot about 5 inches from the end of the string. Thread the end through the ball, run the ball up to the knot, and tie a knot on the opposite side of the ball.
6. Tie the free end of the string to the paddle, through the hole you drilled.

TO PLAY

See how many tries it takes to wind the string completely around the front of the paddle (one loop is made each time you succeed in putting the ball through the hole). It gets easier as the string gets shorter.

A larger version requiring the same skills is **paddle golf**. For it you'll need:
- [ ] a piece of plywood 10 by 6 inches
- [ ] one wooden ball ¾ inch in diameter
- [ ] heavy string 2 feet long

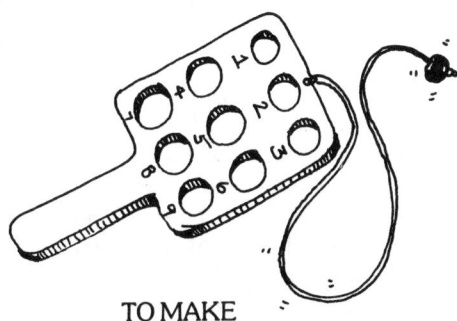

TO MAKE

1. Cut the plywood into a squarish paddle shape having a handle 4 inches long. Round off the corners.
2. Draw 9 holes in rows of three. They should be about ¼ inch larger than the ball. Cut out the holes using a drill and keyhole saw or hole saw in a drill press. Number them 1 through 9.
3. Drill or punch a hole at the center top of the paddle to accommodate the string.
4. Sand all rough edges.
5. Drill a small hole through the center of the ball if it doesn't already have one.
6. Tie a large knot about 5 inches from the end of the string. Thread the end through the ball, run the ball up snug against the knot, and tie a knot on the opposite side of it.
7. Tie the free end of the string to the paddle, through the hole you drilled.
8. Bind the handle with tape over some padding.

TO PLAY

Count the number of tries it takes to get the ball through all of the nine holes in consecutive order. An easier goal is to make the nine holes in any order. Have a friend keep track of your successes and tries.

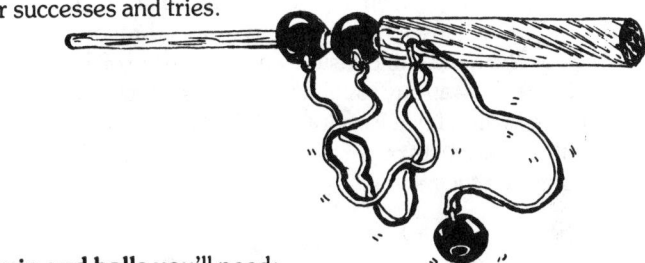

For **pin and balls** you'll need:
- [ ] a 4-inch length of dowel for the handle (1 inch or less in diameter)
- [ ] an 8-inch piece of ¼-inch dowel
- [ ] three 2-inch wooden balls with ½-inch holes through their centers (from a macrame supply store)
- [ ] four small screw eyes
- [ ] three 16-inch lengths of rawhide or other lacing

TO MAKE

1. Drill a ½-inch-deep hole in the center of one end of the handle and glue the ¼-inch dowel piece into it.
2. Put one screw eye in the side of the handle, about ½ inch down from the top. Put one screw eye on each of the balls, about ½ inch from the hole.
3. Insert the end of a rawhide lace through the screw eye of each ball and glue about 1 inch of overlap back on each strand to secure it (clamp with a clothespin while it dries). You may want to reinforce the fastening with several wraps of thread, putting a drop of glue at each end of the thread.
4. Put the loose ends of the three laces through the screw eye on the handle and fasten with an overlap of 1½ inches.
5. Sand away any roughness on the ends of the dowels. If you're feeling festive, paint the handle and balls in bright contrasting colors or personalize your toy with wood-burned designs on the handle.

TO PLAY

Hold two of the balls in your left hand while trying to spear the other. When you succeed, hang onto the remaining ball while trying for the second.

For a **ring version**, get:

- ☐ a stick or dowel about 12 inches long and 1 inch or less in diameter
- ☐ 6 to 8 wooden or metal rings 1½ to 2 inches in diameter (curtain rings or macrame rings)
- ☐ heavy string or leather lacing about 3 feet long

TO MAKE

1. If you use a stick, thin down the top 7 inches with your knife so the diameter is less than that of the handle portion.
2. Carve a shallow groove around the handle, 1½ inches from the end (you'll fasten the string here).
3. Run one end of the string through all but one of the rings and tie it to the last ring.
4. Tie the other end of the string to the handle, snugging it into the groove.

Cup and ball: a very lightweight model in this style can be easily made from an 8-inch piece of small dowel, a small recycled plastic cup-shaped container (save one from hot sauce or mustard, or scrounge in your kitchen drawers), a small wooden bead and a piece of string 16 inches long.

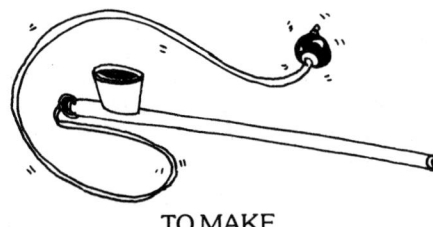

TO MAKE

1. Drill a small hole near one end of the dowel.
2. Use contact cement to fasten the plastic cup onto the dowel as shown.
3. When the cement has dried, run one end of the string through the bead and the other through the hole in the end of the handle, tying knots to secure the string.

BUZZ SAW

This is a humming coordination toy made from a wooden disc threaded on a long double string. The disc is wound up on the string first by flipping it in a circle between the small handles. It is then kept in motion by alternately pulling on and slackening the ends of the string, and as its speed increases, you'll hear the disc humming.

TO MAKE

1. From plywood or other wood about ½ inch thick, cut a disc 2 to 3 inches in diameter.
2. Drill two holes for the string, centered exactly so the disc will be well-balanced. Drill a row of evenly spaced holes around the rim, about ¼ inch in from the edge.
3. Cut two handles 3 inches long from dowel or a branch about ½ inch thick. Shave the middle ½ inch a little so it is thinner than the top and bottom parts of the handle.
4. Cut a piece of strong cord 60 inches long. Thread it through the two center holes as shown, tie the string in a loop, and tie each end of the loop to a handle.

MOUNTAIN BOLO

Two small balls at the ends of a string look simpler than they are. The trick is to get the balls orbiting in opposite directions without running into each other, a feat which takes considerable practice.

TO MAKE

Cut a 38-inch piece of heavy string or nylon line and run each end through a wooden ball about golf-ball size, tying overhand knots on either side of the balls. For a handhold, tie a loop with an overhand knot near the center of the string, but with one cord a little longer. This off-centeredness lets the balls pass each other in motion without touching.

TO PLAY

Hold the string loop with one hand. With the other hand, start swinging the higher ball in a clockwise circle. When it's going steadily, start the other ball going in the opposite direction. It takes a lot of experimenting to learn how to jerk your hand slightly up and down at the right time to keep the balls orbiting.

An easier but still challenging variation can be done with the mountain bolo. Untie the handhold loop and hold the string at its exact center with one hand. With the other, start one ball swinging so that it hits the other. At the moment of impact, jerk the string up a little. This will keep the balls swinging so that they continue to hit each other. See how many swings you can manage without missing!

SIX-SIDED STUMPERS

Eight 1 inch wooden cubes with letters on all six sides are the props for several possible games. Play the ones suggested here and invent more yourself.

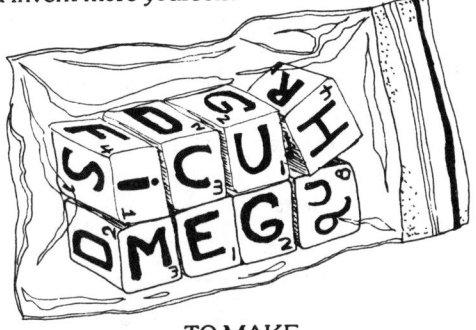

Suggested point values for letters:

a - 1	j - 8	s - 1
b - 3	k - 5	t - 1
c - 3	l - 1	u - 1
d - 2	m - 3	v - 4
e - 1	n - 1	w - 4
f - 4	o - 1	x - 8
g - 2	p - 3	y - 4
h - 4	qu - 8	z - 10
i - 1	r - 1	

TO MAKE

1. Sand eight 1-inch wooden cubes, cut from a 1 x 1.
2. Mark all six sides of each with the letters of different six-letter words. In one corner of each side mark the point value of the letter.

Here are two suggested word lists you might use. Each list has a good variety of letters, some less frequently used, and few duplications.

soaked	fazing	candle	magnum
bounce	victor	zephyr	shower
prowls	jumper	gaiety	bouquet
mighty	turnip	mocked	fields

TO PLAY

There are several ways to play Six-Sided Stumpers:

1. Shake up and roll the cubes, then make the **longest possible word**. Score 5 points for each letter used, taking turns until some player reaches 200 points.
2. Shake up and roll the cubes, then make **as many words as possible** in a given time (say, 5 minutes). Add the point values printed by the letters to get your score.
3. Shake up and roll the cubes, then make one word with the **highest total point values** for the letters.

31

PUT AND TAKE

TO MAKE

Make two small wooden cubes and sand them smooth. Label three sides of one with P and the other three sides with T. On the six sides of the second cube write: 1, 2, 3, 4, A and A. Use something small for counters (such as beans, scales from a cone, or pebbles), giving each player 20 and putting 20 in the pot.

TO PLAY

Take turns rolling the dice, adding or taking counters from the pot according to what you throw. P stands for *put* and T for *take away*. A means *all*. Go four times around the circle, then add your counters to see who has the most.

GAME BOARD

In a 4-inch-square piece of wood about 3/8 inch thick, drill holes of a size to accommodate what you plan to use as markers. Least bulky are shortened matchsticks, some colored with a felt-tipped pen or by dipping in a liquid dye solution. Golf tees work well and can be shortened by ½ inch or so if you like. For Fox and Geese you'll need 17 markers of one color and 1 contrasting one. Migration requires 8 markers in each of two colors; Solitaire is played with 32 markers, any colors.

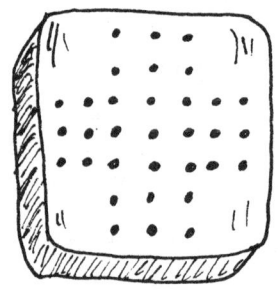

Solitaire (one player)

Put markers in all holes except the middle one. The aim is to remove all markers but one, and the ideal is to have the last marker in the center hole. Markers are removed by being jumped by another marker. Short jumps only (no double jumps) may be made, in any direction except diagonally.

Migration (for two players)

Start with markers laid out as shown. The object is for each player to move all his markers into the holes occupied by his opponent's markers. Moves are made one space at a time or by jumping over a marker to a vacant spot (as in Chinese Checkers). You can use a time limit (how about ten minutes?) or play until one person has all his markers in the other player's territory.

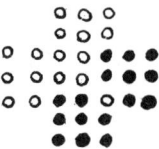

Fox and Geese (for two players)

One player controls the fox and the other controls all 17 geese. The markers are lined up as in the drawing to start the game, with the fox in the hole shown. The fox wins if he catches all but one of the geese; the geese win if they corner the fox so he can't move. Geese have the first move. They can move one space at a time forward from their original position, or sideways to a vacant space. The fox can move one space at a time to a vacant space in any direction except diagonally, or capture a goose by jumping over him to a vacant space (double jumping when possible). When he makes a capture, the goose is taken off the board. The geese can't jump the fox, but must try to corner him so he can't move.

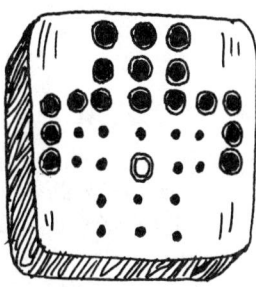

PLANT PRESS

This small but adequate press weighs about one pound and will enable you to transport plant specimens intact and preserve them by drying.

Please show care for the land by collecting only single samples of plants from groups where they are growing well and abundantly.

Materials needed:
- [ ] two pieces of ¼-inch plywood, 6 inches square
- [ ] four 2½-inch carriage bolts
- [ ] four metal washers
- [ ] four wing nuts to fit bolts
- [ ] six pieces of corrugated cardboard, 6 inches square
- [ ] blotter paper cut into twelve or more 6-inch pieces.

TO MAKE

1. Drill holes to fit bolts in the corners of both plywood squares, about ¾ inch in from the edges.
2. Round the corners of the plywood squares and sand all edges smooth.
3. Trim the corners off each piece of cardboard and blotter paper so that when they are stacked between the wood squares they'll clear the bolt holes.
4. Assemble the press by alternating cardboard squares with two pieces of blotter paper and sandwiching the stack between the plywood squares. Put a bolt through each corner, topping it with a washer and wing nut.

WATERSCOPE

Here is a simply made tool for observing and studying all the life and activity going on beneath the surface of the water. It weighs almost nothing, is made from a recycled container, and need not take up much room in your pack, since you can stuff it with socks, a wadded-up hat or your bag of gorp.

Materials needed:
- ☐ an empty one-quart plastic detergent bottle (not round, but one that is flat on two sides)
- ☐ black paint
- ☐ small piece of clear plastic (such as a sandwich baggie)
- ☐ rubber band

TO MAKE

1. Trim off the bottom and top of the bottle as shown, cutting a dip in the middle of one side to accommodate the bridge of your nose.

2. Paint the inside black.
3. When dry, put clear plastic over the open bottom and secure it with a rubber band or sturdy tape.

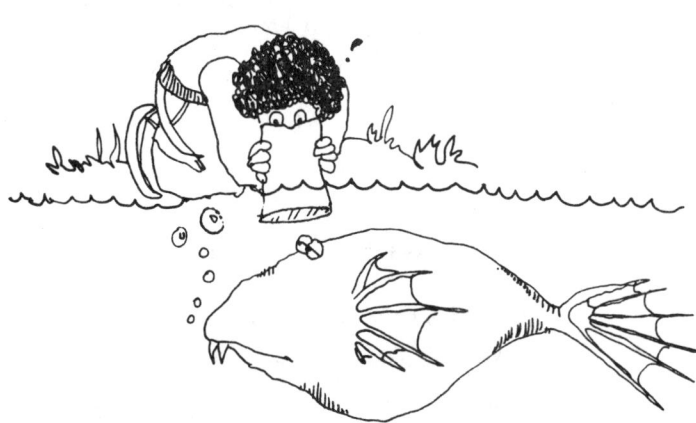

WOOD HARMONICA

The reed in this harmonica is simply a large rubber band stretched between two thin sticks, but with a little practice you'll be able to produce several different notes which will combine into tunes or make a good background for someone else's melody. Tone and pitch can be changed by where you place your mouth, how hard you blow, and squeezing the sticks together.

You'll need:
- [ ] two sticks of wood about 1/8 inch thick, 4½ inches long, 3/4 inch wide
- [ ] one large rubber band to stretch around the sticks
- [ ] two small rubber bands to go around the ends

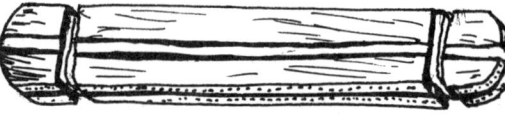

TO MAKE

1. Carve notches near the ends of both sticks to hold the small rubber bands.
2. Sand the sticks smooth.
3. Put the large rubber band lengthwise around one of the sticks, as shown. Secure the sticks together by wrapping the small rubber bands around the notched ends.

ONE-STRING DULCIMER, THE WOODSY SITAR

At seven ounces, this simplified dulcimer is probably the lightest stringed melody instrument you could carry, although it's long enough to require strapping on the outside of most packs. It is played by holding the dulcimer across your lap (or on a log or tent floor) and strumming with one hand while the other presses down on the string between the frets to vary the pitch. This dulcimer has a range of a little over two octaves and is tunable by means of a screw eye to which one end of the string is fastened.

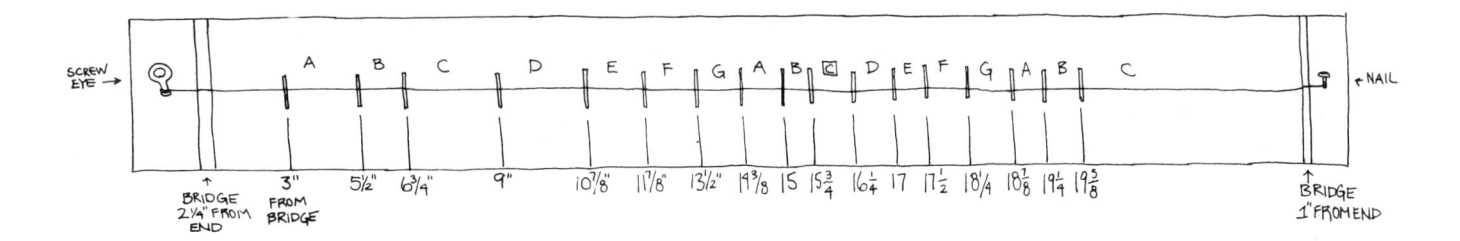

Materials needed:
- ☐ a piece of 1 by 2 board 27½ inches long, pine preferred
- ☐ one medium screw eye
- ☐ one ½-inch nail with head
- ☐ two pieces of ¼-inch dowel 1½ inches long
- ☐ one guitar string (#1 or #2) or very fine wire
- ☐ staples for a household staple gun (3/16 inch)

TO MAKE

1. Sand the cut ends of the long board.
2. Draw lines for placement of the bridge pieces: 2¼ inches from the left end and 1 inch from the right end.
3. Following the diagram, mark the fret lines down the center of the board, measuring from the left bridge line.
4. Set 3/16-inch staples down the neck, one at each fret line. Be as accurate as you can.
5. Install the bridges: flatten one side of each dowel piece and glue that side onto the long board. Clamp till dry.
6. Install the screw eye about 1¼ inches from the left end of the board and centered.
7. Put on the string: through the metal ring at one end of the string, slip a ½-inch nail with a head. Center this nail between the bridge and the right end of the dulcimer.
8. With your pocket knife, make a shallow groove in the middle of each bridge, to keep the string in place as you play
9. Pull the string taut and secure the left end to the screw eye with several turns. When the string is fastened, use the screw eye to adjust it to a good tension for strumming.
10. If you're not used to a fretted instrument, you may find it helpful to put some or all of the note names on masking tape along the neck (see diagram).

37

CROSS FLUTE

The gentle pastoral sounds this simple flute will produce are well worth the patient practice it takes to learn to play. The trick is to blow softly *across* the mouth hole rather than into it. Pitch is approximate, shadings of notes can be made by partially covering the finger holes, and improvisation flows naturally, complete with trills.

TO MAKE

Get about 16 inches of 5/8-inch PVC pipe (from a plumbing supply store) and dig around your kitchen drawers for a cork that will fit inside the pipe.

1. In a straight line, mark for the mouth and finger holes:

    3½ inches from left end of pipe

    4 inches from first mark

    1 inch from second mark

    1 inch from third mark

    1 inch from fourth mark

    1 inch from fifth mark

    1 inch from sixth mark

2. If your workroom is cool, the pipe may be brittle and difficult to drill, so let it sit in a pan of hot water to soften for a few minutes.

3. Clamp the pipe so it won't move while you drill. With a 5/16-inch bit, drill holes carefully at the marks.

4. Mark ¼ inch to the left of the mouth hole. If necessary, shave the cork down so it will fit inside the pipe. Push it in as far as the ¼-inch mark (hammer gently on a short piece of dowel smaller than the pipe if you need more force than your finger can exert).

5. Decorate your woods flute by wrapping bands of colored thread in a few places (glue the ends to secure the thread) or draw on it with indelible felt-tipped pens.

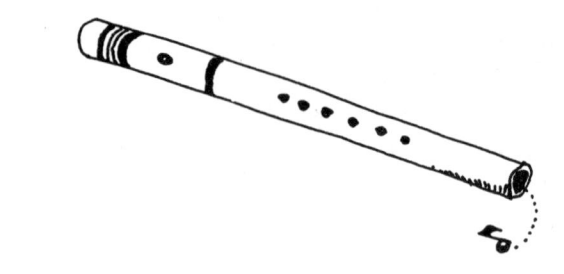

FINGER CYMBALS

Take a few minutes to make these at home and then tuck them in your pack for future tent concerts. They provide a pleasant clicking accompaniment that livens up a song but won't drown it out. If you make two pairs in each size it will expand your rhythm section with slightly different sounds. To play, put a pair on each hand (thumb and middle fingers) and click away!

Materials needed:
- four bottle caps (for tiny cymbals)
- four juice can lids (for larger ones); peel-off lids are best because they have no rough edges and come with a middle bulge
- rubber bands

TO MAKE

1. Flatten the bottle caps with a hammer, then punch a hole in the center of each one with a nail. Tap the hole with your hammer to smooth the edges.

2. Punch center holes in the juice lids and smooth them. down.

3. Place each piece on a board and hit the centers hard with a hammer, to create a slight bulge. When the cymbals are clicked, this space makes a miniature echo chamber.

4. Put a rubber band loop through each hole and fit one cymbal on your thumb and one on your middle finger. Adjust the tension and tie a tight knot in the end of the rubber band that's inside the cymbal, so it won't slip through the hole.

INSTANT ORCHESTRA

The makings for three kinds of impromptu music can be easily tucked into a corner of your pack.

Matchbox harp:
Delightful sounds akin to an African kalimba can be made on even a tiny 1½-inch by 2-inch box, strumming with both your thumbs. A wooden box is stronger than cardboard and you can get fancy and decorate it to add a little charm. Put several rubber bands around an open box and tune them to different pitches by slackening or tightening them.

Strawhorn:
An ensemble of these is probably the lightest-weight orchestra in the world! A strawhorn is strictly a one-note instrument, so you can use them in bell choir fashion, one note to a person. Play simple tunes by tooting your note at the proper time, perhaps coordinated by a director.

Cut the straws into varying lengths so you'll have several pitches (the shorter ones are higher and easier to blow). With fingernails or pliers, flatten out about one inch of one end and crease the sides so the end stays fairly flat. With scissors, trim the flattened end to a V to make the reeds.

Put the V end of the horn between your lips and blow hard. Practice a little to get the best sound, experimenting with the position of the horn and how hard you blow.

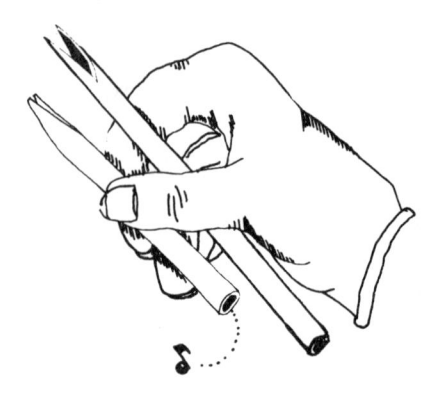

Comb-and-paper kazoo:
Wrap a piece of waxed paper once around your comb so that it makes a fold over the ends of the teeth. Holding the wrapped comb with its teeth pointing up, place your mouth gently over the paper fold and hum through your mouth. By humming a tune you can create sounds similar to a regular metal kazoo.

MOUTHBOW

Another very primitive instrument can be made in the field if you just remember to take along a friend's discarded guitar string and your pocket knife. However, you may want to make it at home if you have access to a particularly good tree branch or sapling. The bow can ride easily lashed to the outside of your pack.

The mouthbow is said to be the earliest musical instrument known and has sung its gentle, haunting song in many cultures. One easy way to play it is to sit down so that you can brace the bottom end on your lap. Hold the bow with your left hand, about 10 inches from the top end. Place the bottom end on your right thigh and the top end against your right cheek near your mouth. The string will be close to your body and parallel to it. Your mouth will be the resonating chamber and you can vary the tones produced by changing the size of the opening. By bending the bow as you play, you can vary the pitch. This is most easily accomplished if you place your left hand on the bow so that your fingers curve over the top and your thumb gives countertension from below (see illustration). Notes are made by plucking or strumming the string with your right hand, using either your fingernail or a plastic pick. A rapid strum will produce the heartiest music, but this takes practice to work up to. Bracing your right forearm against your torso may help.

Materials required:
- [ ] a sapling or tree branch about 3½ feet long, ½ inch wide at one end and slightly larger at the other
- [ ] one guitar string (B if you have a choice)
- [ ] a pick cut from a margarine container

TO MAKE

1. Trim off all twigs so the branch is smooth. Peel the bark if you wish.
2. Cut a groove around the branch about 1 inch from each end, just deep enough to hold the string in place.
3. Put the plain end of the guitar string through the metal ring at the other end to form a loop. Slip this loop around the narrower end of the bow and into the groove.
4. Gently bending the bow into a half circle, pull the string tight and wind the free end of it several times around the larger end, in the groove. Adjust the string tension so that it is secure and firm, then wind the string several times around the straight part of itself and back around the groove. Tuck the end under the wraps and trim off any extra.
5. You might want to fancy up your bow with a feather trim at one end or a design wood-burned on or carved in (shallowly, so as not to weaken the wood).
6. After a few days, as your bow dries, you may need to tighten up the string a little.

Section II:
IN THE FIELD

Here you'll discover dozens of games and other activities to enliven and enrich your wilderness times. The first group is designed to help you tune in to the wilds, observe them closely, learn about them, and feel at home with them. Following this is a collection of games that use mainly your imagination and voice, with no special equipment needed. Next come activities that require a little equipment such as paper and pencil, markers, matchsticks, or playing cards. The last section contains games and activities that make use of your body and your senses. In each section there are many things that can be done in your tent as well as those that need more space and the outdoor elements.

the rock game

TUNING IN TO THE WILDS

Do you get pleasure from noting and studying the terrain, plants and other living beings in the wilds? Is your idea of a *high* coming upon a rabbit form (bed), an owl pellet full of tiny bones, or sighting and identifying a bird you've never seen before? Then you'll probably enjoy testing and stretching your store of environmental knowledge with some of the following exercises. And if you're a hiker who hasn't yet begun to delve into this sphere of wilderness enjoyment, being with those who have may very well make you want to travel to those new horizons — the excitement is contagious.

While hiking, each individual or the whole group together can **make lists** of all the trees and shrubs, wildflowers, birds and mammals they see. You might also want to keep such lists for the area in and around your camps. By far the easiest way for most folks to learn to identify plants and critters is the combination of observing them with someone who has already made their acquaintance and then looking them up in a guidebook.

Agree among your group to **walk silently** for a given period of time or distance. Being quiet and receptive hones all those senses dulled by civilized living, and you'll be amazed at the flood of perceptions coming at you . . . how the bark of different trees feels, the sounds birds make as they scuttle around seeking food, the way the air smells during different kinds of weather. At a rest stop after this interlude, talk with each other about whatever impressed you along the way: sights, sounds, odors, textures, colors, etc. Each of you will be struck by different things, and the sharing will enrich everyone else in the group. This is a fine way to combine the benefits of hiking alone with those of being part of a group.

After the day's journeying is done and the chores of setting up camp completed, find a spot apart from the bustle of other bodies and sit with your eyes closed. **Listen** for as many different sounds as possible, first within the range of a few feet, trying to exclude from your attention all sounds coming from outside that range. Gradually extend your listening zone to larger areas, paying attention to the sounds coming from farther and farther away.

For an **in-depth discovery** of your camping area, divide into lookers, listeners, touchers, tasters, and sniffers. All explore for 20 minutes or so, using the one sense they've chosen. Don't collect anything, but at the end of the time share impressions of your findings.

Go on a nature **scavenger hunt**. Within a square yard of ground (or an approximate such area marked off with extra boot laces or long sticks), find: a sign of man, an animal sign, a plant you can identify, insect and bird signs. Depending on the nature of the terrain, you may want to expand this hunt to a larger area. Also try limiting your search to a more specialized category, such as:

- ☐ **mammal signs** (nibbled cones, bits of hair or fur, a burrow, clawed tree bark, stored seeds, tracks, scats)
- ☐ **bird signs** (nests, empty egg shells, feathers, tracks, holes in trees)
- ☐ **insect signs** (eggs on plants, galls, holes in leaves)

Search out and observe **wildlife in the evening** or night, when most animals are active. Make yourself less obtrusive by wearing dark clothes, mask your scent by rubbing the crushed leaves of a strong-smelling plant such as yarrow or sage over your body and clothes, and (if you're not already grubby enough) smear the exposed portion of your face with charcoal. A flashlight is a big help if you cover the beam end with a piece of red paper or plastic; this will let enough light through to help you see but renders the light a color that most animals perceive as black, or at least don't feel threatened by.

Here's a dandy challenge to **develop your sense of touch**! One hiker finds a rock (fist-sized or smaller) for each member of his clan, remembering where he got them so they can be returned to their natural state after the game. The others sit in a circle with eyes shut. Each is given a rock to get to know by touch *only* (the rockgiver needs to remember who gets which . . . one way to do this is to affix a small piece of tape with the rockee's initial on it). After a few minutes the rocks are collected and redistributed in a different order. Now travelers examine the new rocks by touch and try to recognize their own. If they think they've found their original rock, they keep it; unfamiliar rocks are passed to the person on the right.

Collect feathers. An envelope or small box will preserve them intact. Use your bird book to figure out who used to wear them and study the area to learn whether they were lost during a struggle or by natural molting.

For the more scientific-minded, a **collection of scats** or droppings will expand wilderness knowledge immensely. A good field guide to animal tracks or a book about mammals in your area can help you identify droppings, tracks, and castings (undigested materials such as bones, claws and hair, coughed up by many meat-eating birds and some mammals). This path can lead to curiosity about the critter's behavior patterns and diet, and what plants and other animals inhabit the area. Carefully transported droppings and castings can later be dissected at home with a pair of tweezers, after being soaked in warm water. There you can consult a guide to mammals in the area and try to figure out what the animal ate.

Make an **intensive survey**. Two friends each equip themselves with ten short sticks and a length of line 30 feet or longer which is tied to one of the sticks. Each chooses an area, plants his line-stick and searches for nine objects of interest, making a zigzag path along his line by marking each object with a stick. Partners then take turns sharing their finds and swapping information about them. On a smaller scale, use matchsticks to mark objects in a four-foot plot.

Intensive survey

Bring along two items for making **casts of animal tracks**: a cup of plaster of Paris in a one-quart resealable ziplock type bag, and an inch-deep ring cut from a one quart plastic bleach bottle (or an inch-wide strip of cardboard about 10 inches long and a paper clip to hold it into a ring shape). Caution: label the powder bag so it won't be confused with your food supply! Good tracks can often be found at watering spots such as the edge of a pond or a stream crossing. Gently pick away loose twigs and blow off smaller debris, then press the cardboard or plastic collar into the ground around the track. Pour a little more than ½ cup of water into the bag,

Start a **collection of sketches** of all the animal tracks you come across, identifying and labeling each when possible.

For **studying aquatic life** in ponds and lakes, bring along a homemade waterscope, fashioned from a flat-sided one quart plastic bottle (see Make at Home section, page 35). Peering into the scope you'll witness all the life that teems beneath the water's surface.

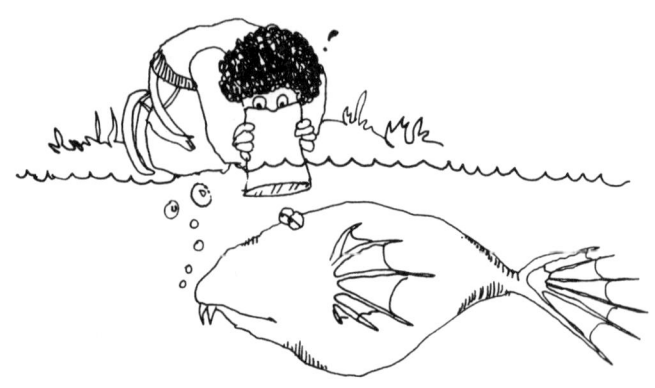

seal it, and mix quickly but thoroughly until the plaster of Paris is about the consistency of buttermilk (you may need to add a bit more water). Carefully pour enough of this mixture onto the track to fill it and cover the rest of the ground inside the ring to about ¼ inch depth. Now sprinkle just a few pieces of grass over the plaster (for a strengthening binder) and add another ½ inch or so of plaster on top of that. After about a half hour the cast will be dry enough to lift away from the ground. Leave the collar on and wrap the whole thing in a paper towel or something else that will protect it on the trip home. There you can remove the collar and clean away loose dirt.

Attract birds for observation by calling in a variety of ways. Some folks become quite adept at whistling mimicked bird calls, but most must content themselves with a squeaky "kiss" on the back of the hand, which simulates a bird's distress or attention sounds. A sound similar to the owl's hoot or mourning dove's call can be produced by cupping your hands and blowing into the hollow forcefully. Try pursing your lips slightly as you blow. A small and inexpensive aid to attracting birds is the Audubon bird call (see catalog section, page 104) which makes a most authentic squeaking sound when twisted.

Go off alone to a spot apart from the rest of your group. Stay there for a time, being as receptive as you can. Record your impressions and/or feelings in **a poem**. Two poetic forms that are well-suited to expressing ideas about nature are *haiku* and *cinquain*, neither of which requires rhyming. A haiku consists of three lines with 5, 7, and 5 syllables. A cinquain is a five-line poem whose lines have one word, then two words, three, four, and five words.

No special equipment is needed for the following games. If someone in the group has a bird or mammal book or a plant guide tucked in his pack, it can be used to check out dubious listings (like consulting a dictionary when playing Scrabble) or to discover, after you've exhausted your fund of stored knowledge, how many more names could fit into your lists. This practice will introduce you to some new wilderness friends and make your lists longer the next time you play.

On solo trips or when there are hours not occupied with conversation and group activity, **make lists** of all the wildflowers, birds and mammals you could recognize on sight.

Either alone or brainstorming in a group, list all the wild plants you can think of whose names **contain animal names** (parrotbeak, spreading dogbane, lamb's quarters).

Think of as many bird names as you can in each of **several categories**, such as birds named for *physical features* (crossbill, horned lark, yellowlegs, spoonbill, purple finch), *area found* (barn swallow, mountain bluebird, sage sparrow), *behavior* (woodpecker, mockingbird, dipper), *sounds* (screech owl, hummingbird, chukar, whistling swan), *diet* (oystercatcher, flycatcher, fish hawk).

HAIKU

High marmot whistles
Alert his sleeping cousins.
Tails retreat in rocks.

CINQUAIN

Snail
Sticky trail
Crosses dead log
Simple journey over leaves
Terminates in aster patch, lunch.

Mammals are much more difficult to list, being of fewer species and, for some reason, having names that don't sort themselves into categories as easily. But perhaps sometime you'll find yourself traveling in the company of some mammal-wise folks who can rise to the challenge of this difficult game. Listen carefully and ponder the possibilities for studying a field new to you. List mammals named for *physical features* (striped skunk, humpback whale, bighorn sheep), *area found* (river otter, prairie dog, ground squirrel), *behavior* (flying squirrel, pack rat, pilot whale).

Stargazing in the wilds can be an exciting and never-ending pursuit, best aided by a traveling companion whose knowledge of the heavens is some steps beyond yours, a pair of good binoculars or small telescope, and a basic book to help you find your way around the sky. *Whitney's Star Finder* (Catalog section, page 105) is small enough to pack along but contains a wealth of information about stars, planets, the sun, moon, meteor showers, how to tell a planet from a star, and much more. Tucked in a pocket in the back is a star finder wheel to enable you to identify what you see in the night sky. Most wilderness goers know how to find Polaris, the north star, are aware of what phase the moon is in when they plan a hike, and relish the crisp, clear panorama above them. Going beyond these basics to more intricate details of celestial activity is deeply rewarding, and a little study will get you there. When perusing the night sky begins to fascinate you, you might start toting a compact telescope (see Catalog section, page 106).

Where will **the sun rise and set**? Knowing how to predict the sun's path is a useful wilderness skill, since this will often have some bearing on how you set up camp. Do you want to catch the first light of day and need the early morning sun to warm camp during breakfast? Maybe the evening's last sun warmth is more important on a particular day. (Once in a while there's the perfect campsite that gathers all the sun you want!) We all know that the sun rises roughly east and sets roughly west of us, but how many of us are so thoroughly aware of its seasonal variations that we feel oriented to the sun by second nature? At the equinoxes (mid-March and mid-September) the sun rises and sets very close to east and west, but between these times its arc varies. In mid-June the sun rises in the northeast and sets in the northwest, and in mid-December it rises in the southeast and sets in the southwest (shortening the days and making for longer

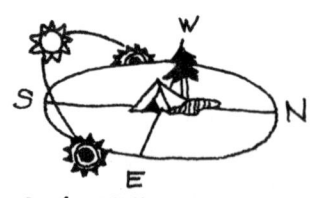

SUN'S PATH MID-JUNE   SUN'S PATH MID-DECEMBER

playtimes in your tent). Take a compass bearing on the setting sun and estimate its rising point by noting the number of degrees difference from west. For instance: Pointing your compass at the sun, you find that it is setting at 252 degrees. This is 18 degrees south of west (270 minus 252 = 18), so you can expect that the sun will rise at approximately 108 degrees (east, which is 90 degrees, plus 18 = 108).

Find north without a compass.
☐ At night, locate the Big Dipper. A line drawn through the two outside stars of the bucket (opposite the handle) and extended about five times the distance between them will meet Polaris, which will be our north star for at least several hundred more years.

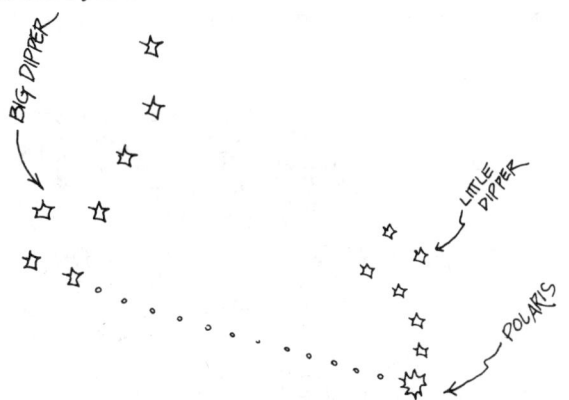

☐ Plant a straight stick in the ground and place a rock, stick, or some other marker at the end of the shadow thrown. Wait 15 minutes and mark the new end of the shadow after it has lengthened. Do this once or twice more, then draw a line through the markers. It will run east-west.

☐ If someone in your group has a watch, use it to find north. If you're in daylight savings time, set the watch back one hour to standard time. Holding the watch level, point the hour hand directly below the sun. North will be at a point on the dial halfway between the hour hand and 12.

How much daylight is left? This is really more important than knowing the exact time in the wilds, since your activities are closely related to the elements and you're living on sun time.

When afternoon is wearing on and you're beginning to think about when to stop walking, where you'll find a likely campsite, or how much time to allow for fixing the evening meal, use this method to get a rough idea of how much light you have left. Extend your arm in front of you with your thumb pointed up and your fingers flat together, palm angled toward you. Move your arm until the sun rests in the corner of the L formed by your palm and thumb. Now observe the distance from there to the point where the sun will disappear (which may be the top of a mountain, the rim of a canyon, or a flat plain) in terms of finger-widths. Each width represents about 15 minutes of daylight left, so if the distance is four fingers it will be approximately one

51

hour until the light dims and the air chills. If sunset is more than an hour away you'll need to enlist the aid of your other hand.

This same method can help you determine morning clock time if you know roughly when the sun rises where you are, didn't bring your watch, and happen to sleep in some morning when you didn't plan to. Do the arm and sun trick toward the easterly sun to figure out about how long it's been up and add that span of time to the time of sunrise to get the current hour.

Expand your **map-reading skills**. If your traveling group includes some folks not yet fluent in the language of topographic maps, some of the more experienced members can devise a few questions and problems to give the novices practice. First, of course, explain the basics of contour lines, colors, and symbols to the beginners. Then, using the map you're hiking with, pose such problems as:

Polallie Creek is a (slow-moving/fast-moving) stream.

Would you carry water on the Paradise Park Trail? Why or why not?

Stump Creek runs (west to east, east to west).

Walking the Skyline Trail from Portage Trail to Ramona Falls is mainly (level, uphill, downhill).

Standing at the East Zigzag Lookout you should be able to see (explain your reasoning for each choice): Tom Dick Ridge / Zigzag River / Slide Mountain / Eden Park / Mississippi Head.

Give a visual description of the Umbrella Falls Trail from Hood River Meadows to the Timberline Trail junction.

GET FRIENDLY WITH YOUR COMPASS

Most backpackers carry one but probably 50% aren't really sure what to do with it, beyond the vague notion that the needle points north. The idea that true north and magnetic north usually aren't the same intimidates many people. They get so discouraged by the adjustments necessary to using map and compass *together* that they never try to learn the simpler and very helpful things a compass *alone* can do. Someone in the traveling group who feels at ease with his compass can guide the others in learning to use theirs, to the satisfaction and benefit of all. It's much easier to practice taking and following bearings out in the wilds than in the confines of a city park, and the benefits of knowing how to use your compass as a tool for travel are clear.

Compasses use somewhat different methods for achieving the same goal — knowing which direction you are going. There isn't space to cover all the alternatives, so the suggestions that follow deal with the basics.

Start out by **explaining the parts** of the compass and their functions: magnetic needle with two ends, fluid-filled housing, dial marked with 360 degrees and cardinal direction points. Make sure everyone understands that the magnetic arrow's only job is to point to magnetic north, and that it will do that faithfully unless diverted by metal nearby. Be sure to check your pockets for magnetic metal such as knives and carabiners. There's a sad story about the traveler who followed his compass for a day only to discover that it was deflected by his belt buckle.

Show how to **orient the compass** so that north on the dial matches north in the field: Align the 360-degree mark under the north-seeking needle. Then set the compass on the ground, being careful to keep it oriented.

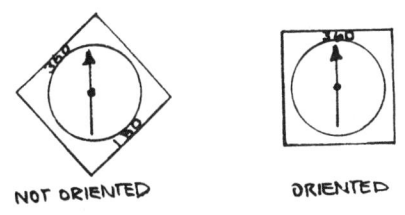

NOT ORIENTED   ORIENTED

Now demonstrate **taking a bearing** to some landmark such as a peak or saddle between two hills. Walk around the compass until the landmark, the center pivot of the compass and your navel are in line and read the bearing where that line intersects the compass dial. Remember the reading!

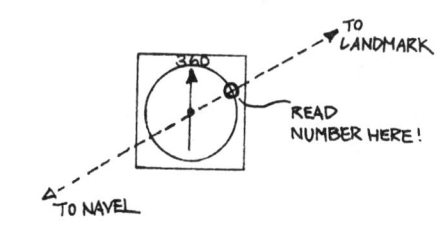

TO LANDMARK
READ NUMBER HERE!
TO NAVEL

The next step is to learn **how to reach a landmark** that will be out of sight after you start traveling toward it. You have determined the bearing to it. Now choose a closer landmark along that same straight line, one that you can keep in sight from your present position (such as a boulder or snag). Put away the compass and travel to the intermediate landmark. Then, to be sure you're headed in the right direction before you choose the next intermediate point, use the compass to orient yourself again . . . hold the compass level in your hand and orient it. Then, keeping it oriented, look down the bearing line you have been remembering. You're facing the original landmark again, even though you can't see it! Pick another landmark along the chosen bearing and travel another leg of your journey. The accuracy of this method of reaching a destination amazes the new learner. Focusing on landmarks helps him feel he's *part* of the scene, not at its mercy.

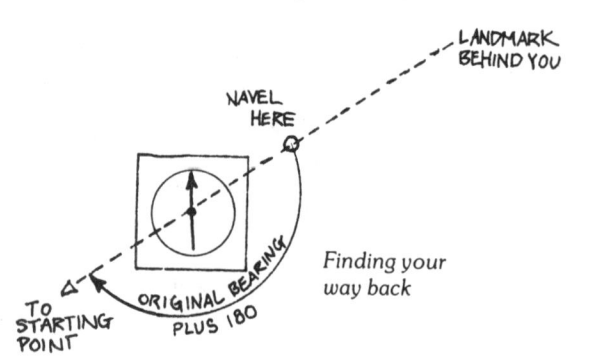

Show that **finding your way back** simply requires heading to the *back* side of the compass circle. That is, just add or subtract 180 degrees (half a circle) from the bearing you followed to get to your destination, and you'll have your "back bearing."

Example: If the bearing was 60 degrees, the back bearing is 240 degrees; if the bearing was 300 degrees, the back bearing is 120 degrees.

A couple of good **exercises for practice** in walking a bearing can be done in a small clearing.

Drop a marker of some kind (smaller than your fist, so you can't see it until you're within a few feet) onto the ground at your feet. Choose a nearby landmark with a bearing of less than 120 degrees. Orient yourself. Put away your compass and walk a given number of paces (say 40 or 50) toward the landmark. Now add 120 degrees to your original bearing and pick a new landmark. Orient yourself and walk the same number of paces toward it as you took on the first leg of your walk. When you've traveled that distance, add 120 degrees to the second bearing, orient yourself, choose a landmark and go the same number of paces toward it. Then search the ground at your feet for the marker you dropped at the start of the journey; if you've been careful, it should be within a foot or two, since you laid out and walked an equilateral triangle!

Finding your way back

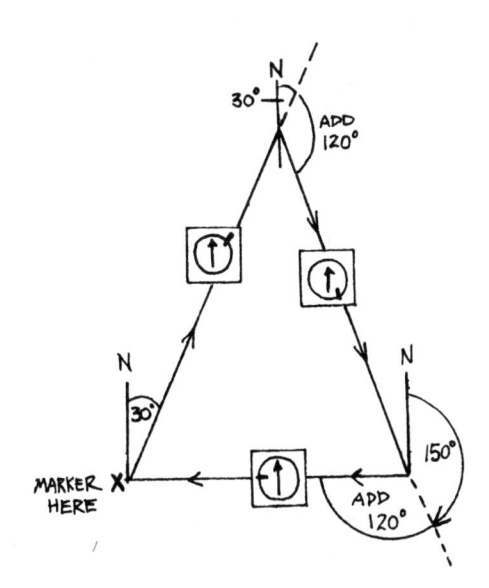

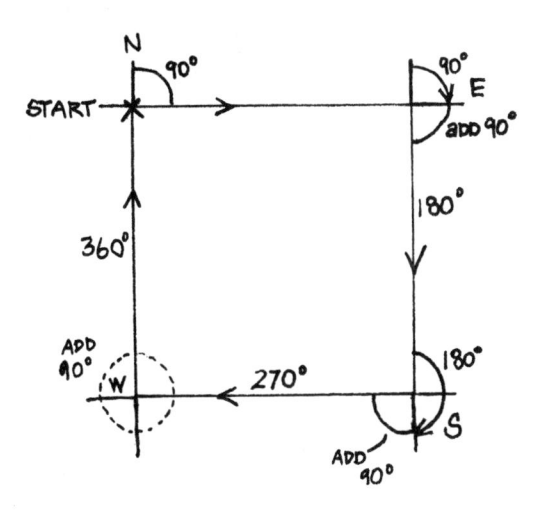

In the second exercise you'll walk a square, using bearings 90 degrees apart, the cardinal points of the compass: east (90 degrees), south (180 degrees), west (270 degrees) and north (360 degrees). Walk the same number of paces on each of the four legs of the journey. First, orient your compass. Look in the direction of 90 degrees on the compass dial and pick out a landmark like a nearby tree or rock. Walk a selected number of paces toward that landmark (say 60 paces). Orient your compass and walk around it so you can sight down 180 degrees. Pick a new landmark. Go the same number of paces, stop. Add 90 degrees to 180 degrees. Orient the compass and get a new sight. Walk. Stop. Orient. Add 90 degrees to 270 degrees. Sight. Walk. Stop. You should be where you started.

55

DARA
(see page 75; ignore one row of boxes)

THE SANDWICH GAME
(see page 74)

NINE MEN'S MORRIS
(see page 75)

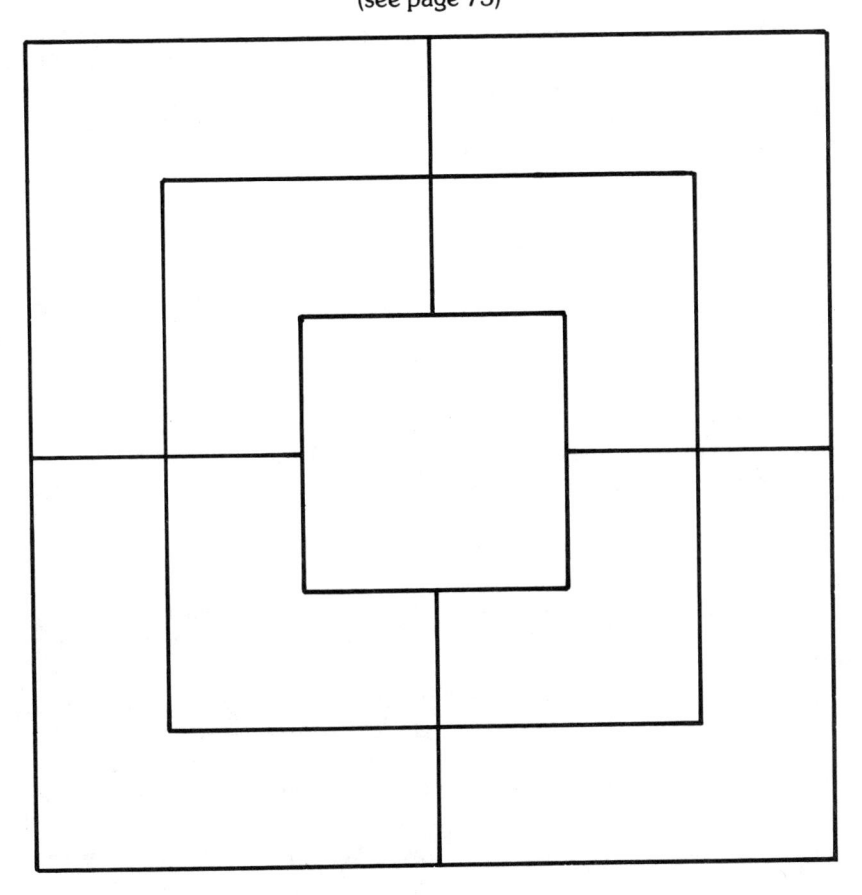

BOLSTERING YOUR BOTANICAL VOCABULARY

As you get friendly with the growing things you'll encounter on hikes, it's fun as well as useful to learn some of the scientific names for plants in addition to the common names they go by. These multi-syllabic designations identify the plant's genus and species and are universally applicable, whereas a given plant may be known by many different common names in different regions. Three hikers who see squawgrass, beargrass, and elk grass are all describing *Xerophyllum tenax*. Cat's ear, mariposa lily, and sego lily are one and the same — *Calochortus subalpinus*.

The scientific name of a plant is usually derived from Latin or Greek words. The first part (genus) describes some characteristic of the group to which the plant belongs. The second part (species) isolates, often with a descriptive term, a feature which defines a subgroup within a genus. So lamb's quarters "formal" name, *Chenopodium album*, breaks down as follows:

Chenopodium = goose foot (describing the leaf shape, from the Greek *chen* meaning "goose" and *podos* meaning "foot")

Album = white (referring to the color of the leaf's underside)

Knowing scientific names is useful in communicating about plants; it also helps you get to know a plant and remember it, clued by physical traits and habitat. For people who enjoy words, it can be great fun and a continuing challenge. There are several ways to expand your botanical vocabulary, both at home and in the wilds.

You might set a first goal of learning the scientific names for **six favorite flowers**.

Go on to a list of the **most common shrubs or trees** in the areas where you frequently hike.

Carry a wildflower book in your pack and use it to make yourself think of the plants you see in terms of their **scientific names only**, as if you were trying to master a foreign tongue. Don't see Queen's cup or bead lily, but rather *Clintonia uniflora*. And isn't *Lysichitum americanum* more intriguing than skunk cabbage?

When you're lounging around camp after dinner, boost your botanical vocabulary with this game:

Using the pared-down dictionary provided on pages 59-61, invent a brief story, substituting a botanical term for an ordinary word whenever remotely possible. Literary license is the key. Ignore the fine rules of definition, grammar, and sentence structure in the interests of working in plenty of botanical terms! Listeners to your tale must try to figure out the meanings of the terms as you go along. When everyone is really stumped, you read the translation.

A BOTANICAL NOVELETTE

Sally, *frigidis* (cold) in this *borealis* (northern) land, put on her *virens* (green) coat and wandered *maritimus* (by the sea). Her heart was *tristis* (sad), her head *suspensa* (drooping). Soon a stranger approached, *formosum* (handsome) and *aristatus* (bearded). Sally's *tremulus* (trembling) heart was *redivivus* (restored). The two were *adnatus* (united), wed *aquatica* (near the water) in an *abbreviatus* (shortened) but *festivus* (festive) ceremony. They rode off *equestris* (pertaining to a horse) to a warmer *australis* (southern) clime, where they grew *matronalis* (sedate, hoary) and *corrugata* (wrinkled) together.

BOTANICAL DICTIONARY

Here is a list of descriptive words I've put together. It may not be totally scientific (even the experts don't agree!), but it's good enough to play with and learn from.

abbreviatus shortened
acephalus headless
acerbus harsh or sour
acris acrid, sharp
acutissimus very acute
adnatus united, joined
adpressa pressed together
aduncus hooked
agrarius of the fields
alata winged
alba white
altissima tallest
amabilis lovely
amoenus charming, pleasing
anceps two-headed, two-edged
aquatica in or near water
arborea treelike, woody
arenarius of sandy places
areolatus pitted or netted
argutus sharp-toothed
aristatus bearded
aromatica aromatic
articulatus jointed
atropurpurea dark purple
attenuata slenderly tapering
aureus golden
australis southern
autumnale autumnal
avicularis pertaining to birds

baccata berried or berrylike
barbatus barbed, bearded
bellus handsome
bicolor two-colored
bicornis two-horned
blandus bland, mild
borealis northern
brachycera short-horned
brevicaulis short-stemmed
brevipes short-footed or stalked
brilliantissimus very brilliant
bullata puckered, blistered

BRACHYCERA: SHORT-HORNED

campestris of fields or plains
canaliculatus channeled, grooved
candidum pure white, shining
canina pertaining to a dog
caprea pertaining to a goat
carnosus fleshy
caudata tailed
caulescent having a stem
celastrus bittersweet
cespitosa in tufts, forming mats
chromatella with color
ciliata margined with hairs, fringed
circinata coiled
coccineus scarlet
comosus with long hair
compactus compact, dense
complexus circled, embraced
confertus crowded, pressed together
cordata heart-shaped
corrugata wrinkled, in folds

crassipes thick-footed thick-stalked
crassus thick, fleshy
crenata toothed, teeth rounded
crinita with long hairs
crispus curled
crustaceous hard and brittle
cucullate hooded
cyaneus blue
cyclops gigantic

dactylifera fingerlike
debilis weak, frail
delicatus delicate, tender
deliciosa delicious
deltoida triangular
diffusus spreading
digitate fingered in a whorl, handlike
diurnus day-flowering
divergens wide-spreading
draco pertaining to a dragon
dulcis sweet

ERIOPHORUS: WOOL-BEARING, WOOLLY.

edulis edible
elongatus elongated
ephemeral lasting one day only
equestris pertaining to a horse
eriophorus wool-bearing, wooly
erosus jagged, as if gnawed
erraticus erratic, unusual, sporadic
eximus distinguished, unusual

fastuasus stately, proud, bountiful
fertilis productive, fruitful
festivus festive, gay, bright
fistulosus hollow, cylindrical
flaccida flabby
flavus yellow
flexilis flexible, pliant
flexuosus zigzag, tortuous
floriferous blooming freely
foetidus fetid, bad-smelling
formosum handsome, beautiful
frigidus cold, of cold regions
fugacious withering quickly
fulgens shining, glistening

glabras smooth, without hairs
glacialis growing on or near a glacier
glutinosus sticky
gracilis graceful, slender
grandiflorus large-flowered

grandis large, showy
graniticus granite-loving
gratissimus very pleasing, agreeable
guttatus spotted, speckled

GUTTATUS: SPOTTED, SPECKLED

hibernalis pertaining to winter
hirsuta with coarse or stiff hairs
hirta hairy

igneus fiery, flame-colored
imbricatus overlapping, as shingles
imperator showy
indivisus undivided
inermis unarmed, without thorns
insignis remarkable, distinguished
intortus twisted

labiata lipped
laciniatus torn, fringed
laevigatus smooth
lanatus wooly

latus broad, wide
littoralis of the seashore
lucidus bright, shining, clear

manicata long-sleeved
marginatus margined or striped
maritimus of the sea or shore
matronalis sedate, often hoary
maximus largest
micans glittering, sparkling
microcarpus small-fruited
minima smallest, dwarf
mirabilis extraordinary
montanus pertaining to mountains
multijuga in many pairs
muralis growing on walls
mutabilis variable

nanus dwarf
natans floating, swimming

NATANS: FLOATING, SWIMMING.

nemoralis of groves or woods
nobilis noble, famous
noctiflora night-flowering
nocturnus of the night
nudatus nude, stripped
nutans nodding

ocellata with small eyes
officinalis medicinal
orbiculatus round
ornatus adorned

pallidus pale
palustris growing in the marsh
parviflorus small-flowered
parvum small
patulus spreading
pauciflorus few-flowered
peregrinus exotic, foreign
phaeus dusky
picta painted or variegated
pileatus with a cap
placatus quiet, calm
plena double, full
plumarius plumed, feathered
ponderosus heavy, massive
praecox precocious, very early
pratensis of meadows
princeps princely, first
procumbens trailing, prostrate
prolifera many-leaved
ptarmica sneeze-producing
pungens piercing, sharp-pointed

redivivus restored, brought to life
refractus broken
repens creeping
retusa notched
rigens rigid, stiff
rivalis pertaining to brooks
rostrata beaked
ruber red, ruddy

saccatus baglike
salinus salty, of salty places
sapidus savory
saxatilis found among rocks

SAXATILIS: FOUND AMONG ROCKS

scandens climbing
secundus side-flowering
semperflorens ever-flowering
senilis old, white-haired
serotinus late-flowering
spendens splendid
suspensa drooping
sylvaticus forest-loving

tenax tenacious, strong
tremulus quivering, trembling

tristis sad, bitter, dull
trivialis common, ordinary

uliginosus of wet or marshy places
urens burning, stinging
utilis useful

vacillans swaying
validus strong
vegetus vigorous
velutinus velvety
vernalis of spring
verrucosa warty

VERRUCOSA: WARTY

virens green
vittatus striped
vulgaris common

xanthinus yellow
xeranthemum everlasting

61

MIND AND MOUTH GAMES
(no special equipment needed)

TWENTY QUESTIONS

Play this old favorite with a wilderness twist by limiting the mystery item to something present in the tent or camp, or something encountered in the day's hiking. The person chosen to be It thinks of a mystery subject and tells the others its general locality and whether it is animal, vegetable, or mineral. Each player in turn can ask one yes/no question, to get clues or to guess what the subject is. If someone guesses the subject correctly, he gets a turn at being It. If the twenty allotted questions are all used up before anyone can solve the mystery, It wins. He then tells the group the answer and has another go at stumping them with a new subject.

WORD PAIRS

The last word of a pair becomes the first word of the next pair. For example: First player says "lunch box" and second player says "box spring." When one player is stuck, he says a new pair of words and then drops out.

ENDLESS CHAIN

The first player says a place name (it's usually more fun to limit these to places a hiker might go, rather than include cities and countries). The next player gives another place name that *begins* with the *last* letter of the first-named place. For instance, your chain might go like this: Three Fingered Jack/Kaleetan Butte/Elk Meadow/Windigo Pass/Snake River.

Other variations of this game use names of plants, birds, or animals (how about adding sound effects to the latter?). *Plant chain*: stinging nettle/elderberry/yarrow/watercress. *Birds*: kingbird/dipper/raven/nuthatch. *Animals:* marten/nutria/antelope/elk.

NAME STRETCH

This one takes a lot of imagination and allows for much literary license. Take place names chosen from your hiking map. You might want to write them on slips of paper and toss them in somebody's hat; each player uses the one he draws.

Each person works a place name into a sentence, such as (for Santiam), "I *sent a yam* to market." In the most challenging form of this game the group tries to carry on a conversation, choosing names from their map and making up sentences that can be interrelated.

SING OUT

The leader gives each player a word and one minute to think of a song in which that word appears. After the minute is up, the person must sing a line from his song.

GRANNY'S BACKPACK

This variation on the old Grandmother's Trunk theme can use any kind of outdoorsy words (most fun) or limit words to certain categories such as animals, food, people (more difficult). First player, "I looked in Granny's backpack and I found (*name an item starting with the letter A*)." Second player, "I looked in Granny's backpack and I found (*first player's word* and *something starting with the letter B*)." Successive players repeat in order all the words already given and add one for the next letter of the alphabet. For a tougher version use an adjective and a noun starting with the same letter: "an agile antelope, a brusque bear, a cautious coyote, a dubious dingo . . ."

SENTENCED

The first player gives a word with no more than eight letters, and the second player responds with a sentence whose words begin with the letters of the starter word, in order. You might want to limit starter words to outdoor-related terms.

Here are sample exchanges:
COMPASS: "Climbing On Mountains Pleases A Sturdy Soul."
STOVE: "Serena Tripped Over Victor's Earthworms."

In a variation of this game the starter word can be of any length but the second player must answer with only outdoorish words (single words, not forming a sentence).

BOOTS: Backpack, Osprey, Overeat, Tarn, Summit.
CHIPMUNK: Crevasse, Hammock, Insect, Parka, Map, Underwear, Nettles, Knife.

The most difficult starter words are long ones with some double letters.

WATT ZYNONYM?

The object of this brainstorming game is to devise names with hidden meanings, tacking a quirky last name onto a legitimate first name, such as Sheila Rainjit (*she'll arrange it*):

Lyle Little
Morris Better
Carol Ott
John Diss
Joan Yeronordijarennet

Chad Aheddake
Blaine Truth
Justin Tyme
Drew Conclusions
Hedda Lettuce

CARTOGRAPHER'S DELIGHT

See if you can name all your state's counties, major rivers or mountains, or state parks/wilderness areas.

HIG-PIG

One person gives the definition of a pair of rhyming words, usually a noun and its adjective. The pairs can have one syllable each (a hig-pig), two syllables each (a higgy-piggy) or three syllables each (a higgety-piggety, and durn difficult!). Along with the definition clues, you must tell the guesser which form it is. For instance, "crimson cot" is the clue for the hig-pig *red bed*. A higgy-piggy defined as "a far-out primate" is a *funky monkey*. And the clue "sour group" defines the higgety-piggety *astringent contingent*. Your crowd may contain a wordsmith who goes for four-syllable pairs: "a person from Southern Germany who works with books" is a *Bavarian librarian*.

TONGUE TANGLERS

Tongue twisters have been around for generations; it's believed they originated as elocution exercises for hapless schoolchildren. Twisters are still great fun to tackle and a genuine challenge to create.

Try rolling these **old standbys** trippingly off the tongue several times in quick succession:
Does this shop stock socks with spots?
The sixth sheik's sixth sheep's sick.
A big black bug bit a big black bear and the big black bear bled blood.
A skunk sat on a stump. The skunk thunk the stump stunk and the stump thunk the skunk stunk.

Build a progression of **alliterative sentences** around a circle of players, each repeating the sentences before his and adding a new one of his own creation. For example, your bunch could start its sentences with *numerals*:

One overweight ox obsequiously offering olives.
Two trembling tapdancers timidly tripping to town.
Three triumphant troubadours trouncing truculent
    trumpeters.
Four frantic floorwalkers feverishly frisking Florence.
. . . and so on!
The challenge is heightened by repeating each sentence quickly three times.

Other possibilities for sentence starters:

Colors	Yes, yellow yaks yield yardage to yelping yearlings yearning for yams.
Names	Bertha boggled bleary-eyed buffoons by blithely beckoning brash blacksmiths.
Weather words	Thunder thrills the trilling titmouse.
Places	Pennsylvania's placid playgrounds promise plentiful pranks to prolific poets.

Thunder thrills the trilling titmouse

WHAT AM I?

One person goes out while the rest of the crew decides what animal he'll be. He comes back and tries to learn his identity by asking questions that can be answered yes or no. To add a little pressure, set a time period or limit the number of questions.

I'M THINKING OF . . .

A turned-around version of What Am I has everyone trying to guess what one person has in mind, asking only yes/no questions. The person decides on his mystery subject and tells the group, "I'm thinking of (a person who wrote a book/a person who traveled a great distance/a pioneer/an animal)." It is most challenging if the original clue is obscure; for instance, *the person who wrote the book* is not usually thought of as an author.

LISTS GALORE

Challenge your friend with a heading from which he makes the longest possible list. You might start out easy with **famous animals:** Moby Dick, Trigger, Lassie, Morris, Barrie (the first rescue dog). Go on to animals with horns, books with four-word titles, things you can see through, ways to cross a river, vehicles without wheels, uses for a bean, things you can do while hanging onto your ears with both hands, objects that work only in pairs. It's as much fun to invent the categories as it is to think of crazy items for the lists.

BOIL THIS DOWN

Challenge each other to guess titles of books, movies, television programs by telling stories which give clues. Tell the guessers which category the mystery title is in.
　　This example hides the title of a TV program: A man going home to a family reunion at Thanksgiving missed his plane. When he finally arrived several hours late there was no dinner left. He asked his mother where the food was and Mom replied, "It's _____ (*All in the Family*)."
The film title *Silent Running* might be disguised in an intricate story about a mugger in tennis shoes.

GAMES THAT NEED A LITTLE EQUIPMENT

WORD GRID

The group chooses a word whose letters are written vertically down the left margin of each person's paper. Across the top make column headings for categories such as animal, flower, food, mountain, book title, city, etc. The aim is to fill in each space after the key word's letters with entries in each category, choosing the most unusual words you can think of. Set a time limit.

More points are given for words least used by the group. For example, if six are playing, there'll be a maximum of six points for each space. If only one player uses a word no one else does, he gets six points for that box. If two players use the same word, or two use different words that no one else enters, each gets three points. If all six players use the same word in a spot, each gets one point.

Here is a sample grid to show you how it might go and, obviously, choosing a key word with double letters stretches the players' resourcefulness:

	animal	plant	food	mountain
B	BADGER	BUNCHBERRY	BULGUR	BROKEN TOP
O	OPOSSUM	OCEAN SPRAY	OATMEAL	OLALLIE BUTTE
O	OCELOT	OREGON GRAPE	OCTOPUS	ODELL
T	TOWNSEND'S MEADOW MOUSE	TWAYBLADE	TORTILLA	TUMALO
S	SPERM WHALE	SPIREA	SHRIMP	STRAWBERRY

POINTS FOR PAIRS

Each person is given the same list of pairs of letters (for instance: PT, NQ, EF, XE, NK). A time limit is set and players list words which contain the letter pairs.

There are several possible variations of this game:

1. Using the *shortest* possible words, give one word for each pair.
2. Use the *longest* word you can think of for each pair.
3. First think of at least one word for each pair, then fatten out your list with **all the others** that come to mind.
4. Play this basic game with groups of **three** letters instead of pairs (ABA: abase, calabash, crabapple; SAG: message, saga, lasagna).

KEEP YOUR EYES PEELED

One player comes into the group, wearing as many things as possible besides his usual attire (he might add compass, binoculars, walking stick, sunglasses, poncho). The rest of the group is told to watch him carefully and note what he *does*. He can use his imagination in doing things to throw them off the track, then go out of sight. Group members are *then* told to write a list of what he wore. The longest list wins, and there's a penalty of one point for each incorrect listing.

ONE MINUTE OF WORDS

Choose a letter. Each person writes as many words as possible beginning with that letter. Someone watches the time and calls when one minute is up.

To increase the difficulty of this game, choose a less common letter such as J, V, K or Q, limit words to four letters or more, and rule out plurals, proper nouns, and different tenses of the same word. If your group is a really wordy one, you might cut the time limit down to 30 seconds to put the pressure on.

DERIVATION

Someone thinks of a long word (how about mountainous, irridescent, topographic, or unforgettable?). The players write it down and, in an agreed time limit, each makes as many new words as possible out of the letters it contains. Limiting words to four or more letters increases the difficulty of the game.

QUICK CHANGE

Players are given a list of words and their opposites (or play with any kind of word pairs). The goal is to change the first word to its opposite in the fewest number of operations by adding, dropping, or changing one letter at a time in the word. Score one point for each change, with the lowest total score in the group winning. Here's the way it's done:
  WET to DRY: wet, bet, bat, bay, day, dry — 5
  HOT to COLD: hot, cot, colt, cold — 3

PROFILES

Each person draws a profile of the friend to his right (set a two-minute time limit). The subject's name is written on the back of each drawing, then all the pictures are mixed up and rearranged, face up, on the tent floor. Each person tries to pick out his own likeness.

EXPANSION

Everyone is given the same list of five or more short words, and a time limit in which to make a new word from each of them. The first new word is formed by adding one letter anywhere in the word. Then, to that word, a player adds another letter to make another new word. New letters are added one at a time to make as many additional words as possible. Ruling out plurals makes this game more difficult.

When the time limit is up, players find their scores by

counting the number of letters they were able to add to the original list of words.

Here are a few examples:

rain, train, strain	2
pin, pint, print, sprint	3
ire, tire, tired, tiered	3
ran, rant, grant	2
are, pare, spare, sparse	3

WEAVE-A-WORD

Two or more players each draw a five-square grid. The first player calls out any letter and he and the others write it in any one of their boxes. The next player calls out another letter which everyone enters in his grid, and so on until 25 letters have been called and each person's grid is filled. There are no restrictions on the letters called, so there may be repeats. The goal is to place the letters in your grid so as to spell as many words as possible in all directions: horizontally, vertically and diagonally. No proper nouns allowed!

To score: count 10 points for a five-letter word, 5 points for a four and 3 points for a three. Count the *longest* word, not the words within it. Once a letter is entered in a box, it can't be moved around. To give everyone a good chance, keep score for several games in a row.

TRIANGLE CAPTURE

Draw a triangular grid of dots with at least eight to a side. The players take turns drawing connecting lines between two adjacent dots; the goal is to completely close a triangle. When someone does fill in a triangle, he writes his initial inside and must take another turn, even if it sets his opponent up for a successful capture. When all the dots have been connected, the player with the most triangles wins.

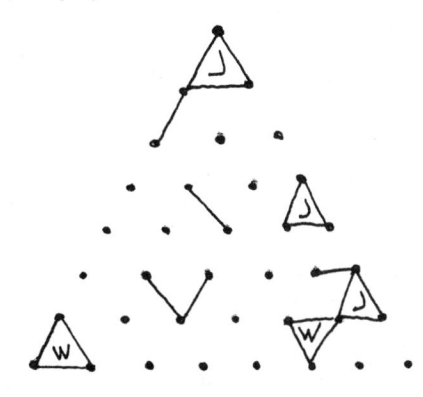

NUMBER TIC TAC TOE

Instead of X's and O's, play with numerals. One player uses 2, 4, 6, 8, 10 and the other uses 1, 3, 5, 7, 9. Each player in turn writes any of his numbers in any space on a three by

71

three grid, using each number only once. The winner is the first person to complete a row in any direction that totals 15 (this might include opponent's numbers). Try playing for other totals up to 20; the higher totals are more difficult.

WHIMSICAL WORD WEAVING

Tickle your mind and tongue with zany images by weaving as many rhymes, alliterations, and subtle transitions as possible into a screwy story with a bare, unlikely thread of plot. This is most easily accomplished with paper and pencil so you can jot down the words that flit through your mind, one leading to another. Get a fat collection of words together, then free-associate a story that incorporates them in a mirthful manner. Here's a sample of what you might produce with a few minutes' pondering:

> Tarrying, Hairy Harry stared warily at Merry Mary's hirsuite malamute Hugh. Astutely, Harry stared at the cute suit Merry Mary wore. But for its hue and shape, her suit could be another hirsute malamute or an ape. Thickly furry, Merry Mary's suit shared with her hirsute malamute Hugh huge hunks of murky mange. "Strange," murmured Hairy Harry to Merry Mary, "that you should make merry despite a mangy malamute and suit."

STORY BALL

Gather the extra bootlaces and odd bits of line that group members have in their packs, and wind up a ball of differing length pieces tied together (cut a few short pieces to include in the ball). One person holds the ball and begins inventing a story while slowly unwinding the line, running it through his fingers. When he reaches the first knot he stops and passes the ball on to the next person, who picks up the story and continues spinning the tale while unwinding the line. This yarn-spinning continues on around the circle until the whole ball is unwound and a complicated plot has been hatched, embellished, and hopefully brought to a tidy conclusion.

TEAMWORK TALES

In this model of joint storytelling, the tale is built one sentence at a time by each player in the circle. It may grow to epic proportions when the creative muse is present and participants gleefully set up their co-narrators with tough sentences to follow.

TWO-SIDED DICE

In many ancient games sets of sticks were tossed to

determine points. Bones, shells, stones, and sticks were decorated and/or carved to distinguish two different sides (often one rounded, one flat). The player's score was determined by the combination of sides landing up in his throw. Usually each player had at least five pieces. The game could be elaborated by carving the sides in two different designs, such as four stars and one moon or three hawks and two turtles. Scoring was determined according to the likelihood of throwing given combinations.

The simplest form is playing with five sticks which are white on one side and black on the other. One point is given for each white side landing up. Tallies might be kept by the use of small counter sticks or pebbles, or by moving a tally stick along a series of holes in the ground.

Here are three possibilities for two-sided dice:

1. Small cowrie shells, 10 or 15 cents each at lapidary or jewelry supply stores (score according to how many open sides land up).

2. In the field, carve two-sided sticks this way: Find sticks ½ to 1 inch in diameter and 3 or 4 inches long. Split them lengthwise with your pocket knife, peel off the bark and carve designs on the rounded **or** the flat sides (all on the same side).

3. At home, saw lengthwise down the middle of pieces of dowel ½ inch in diameter. Make the pieces 3 to 4 inches long. Sand them smooth and carve either the flat or rounded sides or paint them in two contrasting colors.

Two-sided dice

MATCH GAMES

Here are two versions of an age-old pickup pastime. Either can be played by simply laying out patterns of matchsticks, stones, coins, etc.

In the first game, pieces are arranged in a triangle. Two players alternate picking up pieces. A player can pick up as many as he wants from any horizontal row, but from only one row at a turn. The object is to make your opponent pick up the last piece.

The second game is played with pieces arranged in a rectangle of any size (for instance, eight across and five down). Players take turns picking up any number of pieces from any row or column, but *only* pieces that are adjacent to each other. For example, if one player picks up the top four pieces from the third column, the other can't pick up any of the complete first four horizontal rows because there are gaps in them. He *can* pick up the whole fifth row (because it has no gaps) or any number of adjacent pieces on the broken rows. The player to pick up the last piece wins.

Match Game - 1

Match Game - 2

These three games can be played on the boards printed in the center of the book, pages 56-57.

THE SANDWICH GAME (for two players)

In the city you'd use 18 pennies for each player, one using heads, the other tails. Since you're not likely to have those in your pack, take cardboard circles either colored on one side or marked H on one side and T on the other. The game is played on a grid six squares by six squares (see page 56).

Start with four "pennies" in the center, thus:

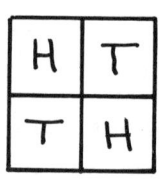

Take turns putting down a penny, trying to sandwich your opponent's pennies between two of your own. When you succeed, turn over the ones you sandwiched so they become yours. You can sandwich horizontally, vertically, diagonally, in two directions at the same time, and more than one penny at a time. When the board is full of markers, tally the number of heads and tails to see who wins.

DARA (for two players)

This African game can be played on a grid of five by six holes scratched in the dirt, or on paper (ignore one column of our six-square grid on page 56). Each player has 12 pieces all one color (pebbles, beans, candies, etc.).

There are two parts to the game. In the first each player takes turns putting his men, one at a time, on the board. The only limitation is that he can't put more than two next to each other. In the second part of the game players take turns moving their men, one space at a time in any direction except diagonally (no jumping allowed). The object is to get three men in a vertical or horizontal row. When a player succeeds, he can remove one of his opponent's pieces. The game is over when one player can't make any more rows of three or when all of one player's pieces have been removed.

NINE MEN'S MORRIS (for two players)

Similar to Dara, this game is over 3,000 years old! It is played on a different grid (see page 57) and each player has nine pieces. The players take turns placing pieces on the board at corners or where lines intersect, one at a time. When one person gets three in a row (horizontally, vertically, or diagonally), he can remove one of his opponent's pieces, but not from an already formed row of three unless there are no others to take. When all nine markers have been placed, continue the game by moving to *adjoining* spots, trying to make lines of three.

A player wins by capturing all but two of his opponent's pieces, or else blocking so the other person can't move anywhere. It is all right to move one of your pieces out of a line of three already formed, then move it back on your next move to form a "new" line of three.

PUZZLES FOR YOUR FINGERS (answers at the end of this section)

1. If you sawed up a painted cube with six even cuts as shown, how many mini-cubes would have three painted sides? How many two painted sides? How many only one?

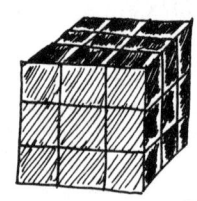

2. A person has 20 coins, all dimes and quarters. If his dimes were quarters and his quarters were dimes, he'd have 90 cents more than he now has. How many dimes and how many quarters does he have?

3. Arrange ten small objects (coins, pebbles, cones, candy) in a pyramid. Try to reverse the pyramid by moving only three.

4. The Volga Boatman: Marco Polo started for China with a rabbit, a fox, and a head of cabbage. When Marco came to the Volga River, he got the last rental boat. It could carry only him and one other object. If left alone, the fox would eat the rabbit and the rabbit would eat the cabbage. How did he get everything across the Volga intact?

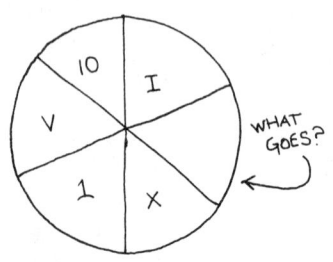

5. Complete the circle. What goes in the empty space?

6. Magic Fifteen: This problem can be tackled by a lone trekker or by several friends. Each person draws a grid three squares by three squares and fills the nine boxes with the numbers 1 through 9, using each number once. The object is to arrange the numbers so that each row, column and long diagonal adds up to 15.

7. Which two words in the English language have the five vowels in successive order?

8. There are seven amoeba in the bottom of a jar, and they multiply so fast that they double in volume every minute. If it takes 40 minutes to fill the jar, how long would it take to fill it half full?

Stick puzzles (use matches or small sticks the same size)

9. Arrange eight sticks in a pattern that includes two squares and four triangles.

10. Arrange twelve sticks as shown and move only three to get three squares.

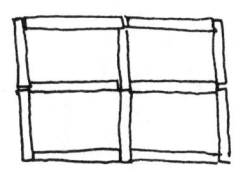

11. Lay out seven sticks in this triangle and then change the pattern to three connecting triangles by moving four sticks.

12. With sixteen sticks, make the following pattern. Then move only three sticks to get four boxes.

13. Take five sticks away from this figure to leave five triangles.

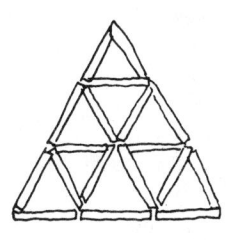

14. Arrange three matches in a triangle without having any match heads touch the table.

77

CARD GAMES

ALBANIAN DWARFS (for three or more players)

The object of this game is to get rid of all your cards. The dealer gives each player seven cards and puts the rest in a pile face down in the middle, turning up the top card and placing it beside the pile.

The face-up card determines the play: a player must play on top of it a card of the same number (this will change the suit) or suit from his hand. If he can't play, he must draw one card. In addition, if certain cards are face up, he must draw from the pile instead of being able to get rid of a card. If an ace is up, he draws one card. If a 2 is up, he draws two cards. If a 3 is up, he draws three cards. If a 4 is up, he skips his turn. If a jack is up, he reverses the direction of play around the circle, with the player to his right taking the next turn. When someone plays his next-to-last card, he must say "last card" so that the other players can do their best to prevent him from going out.

SPOONS (for three or more players, the more the better!)

In addition to a deck of cards, you'll need several small similar objects for this game, such as spoons (one fewer than the number of players). Pocket knives, pens, lip balm, or candies will work fine. Place the objects in the center of the circle of players, where everyone can reach them. At one point in the game there'll be a quiet but mad scramble to draw a spoon, and the object is not to get left without one.

The dealer passes out four cards to each player and puts the rest of the pile face down beside himself. Each player tries to gather four of a kind in his hand, by passing on cards he doesn't want and keeping ones he does, always holding a total of four cards. The dealer starts the card-passing by drawing from the pile. If he likes what he picks up, he keeps that card and passes one of his others, face down, to the player on his left. If he doesn't like his draw, he simply passes on that card. The next player judges each card he is passed and either keeps or passes it on also. Of course, this gets very hectic and isn't done one neat card at a time, because everyone is in a hurry to be the first with four of a kind in his hand.

When this happens, the player can draw a spoon from the center. He tries to do this quietly and casually, because this action allows the other players to draw a spoon also. One person gets left without a spoon, the loser for the round. To mark his loss, he writes down one letter of the word SPOON (or whatever object is being used). Each loss adds one letter to a player's word. When someone has tallied enough losses to spell the whole word, he's out of the game. When the game gets down to two players, the one with the least number of letters is declared winner.

SPEED (for two players)

The object of this fast-paced game is to get rid of all your cards first. Success depends on alert eyes and quick hands!

The dealer puts down in a row, face down: five cards in one pile, then one card next to it, one card next to that, and another pile of five. He then deals the rest of the cards equally to the players.

Each player puts his pile face down in front of him and draws four cards from it for his hand. Throughout the game, keep replacing the cards you play from this stockpile so that you have four in your hand.

Simultaneously each player turns over one of the single cards in the center. Both players can play on both these cards (to the swift goes the victory!), playing either one card higher, one card lower, or the same number in the opposite color. Play continues in the same manner as new cards are laid down, until neither player can play on either card. Then each person simultaneously turns over a new card from the pile of five to his right, and play continues.

When the piles of five are used up, turn the center stacks of cards over, push them to the sides and turn two new cards up in the center. The game ends when one player gets rid of all his cards.

TWITCH (for two players)

An all-stops-out game of Twitch has been known to end in a deck of bent cards and two extremely high levels of adrenalin. This is a fine contest of quick reflexes. The goal is to get rid of all your cards before your opponent does.

Divide all the cards between the two players. Don't look at your cards! Each player lays out five cards, face down in a row in front of him, so that there are two aligned rows of five.

Starting at the same end, each player turns one card face up. Disregard suits and look for pairs. If the two cards make a pair, play a card from the pile in your hand (face up) to cover each of the matching cards — FAST! If the two cards turned up *don't* make a pair, then turn over the next two in line. Scan all the face-up cards for matches and play on as many as you can. As more cards are turned face up, occasionally there'll be three of a kind showing and you should try to play cards on all three.

When the whole line of five has been turned up and no more plays can be made, pick up the cards from the row on your side, put them in your hand, and lay out five more as you did at the start of the game. Continue playing until one person has managed to play all his cards.

BODY AND SENSES GAMES

Juggling materials abound in the wilds: small stones, pine or fir cones, sock balls made by wadding up your footwear (preferably the clean ones). Juggling three things at once is a challenge to the individual, but so is a group juggle, with two facing lines of friends keeping several items airborne.

Get up a **grass-blowing** ensemble, making music on blades of grass held taut between your thumbs. The pitch will vary with the width of the blade and how tightly it's held.

Sleeping Giant can be played day or night. Let your imagination find hidden objects in the shapes of natural things such as clouds, trees, rocks, or a range of hills. When your bed is under the stars, use the silhouettes of trees and landforms as your springboard for flights of fancy.

Blow bubbles (biodegradable camp suds work fine) using cupped hands, a paper cup with a small hole punched in the bottom, or a straw (held horizontally, this will produce a quick flood of small bubbles). Have a contest: who can blow the biggest bubble? whose will travel farthest?

Pitch pennies or cards into a pan or somebody's hat from several feet away. More difficult: use a water bottle as the target and toss straight sticks or chopsticks into it. Try giving each player ten throws.

Whittling and wood carving can soothe the mind and bring out the artist in you. A small figure you've sculpted with a pocket knife on a summer hike becomes a treasure under someone's Christmas tree. If the project goes awry, just turn it into a fuzz stick to start the evening campfire.

Fly a lightweight, packable **kite** from a mountaintop or clearing, taking care not to be hard on the land. (See the Catalog section, page 104, for some mail-order kite suppliers.)

Collect a few special things to take home and weave into a wall hanging: twigs with unusual shapes, a bright piece of lichen, a bit of bark with an interesting texture, a feather — anything whose removal won't diminish the environment. Bind them together with coarse yarns in natural colors. Small pieces of wood found on your hikes can be glued into a frame for a collage to warm your memory.

OOOOH — AAAAH:

Pass a hand squeeze around a circle, accompanied by an Ooooh. Start an Aaaah squeeze going in the opposite direction. Eventually someone will get both at once. To stir things up, try reversing the direction every so often.

HONE YOUR SENSES:

There are several ways to play this basic game of identifying objects by calling into use senses other than sight. Players are blindfolded for all.

In the **tasty** version, the sightless player is presented with eight or ten edibles which he tries to identify. Don't let him touch them, but give him a nibble of each.

Smell and Tell challenges the guesser with several items, both edible and inedible, for identification via sniffing only.

The Touching Test allows the player only to feel objects to determine what they are.

Another twist on this basic theme tests both senses and memory. Blindfolded players sit in a circle and a leader quickly passes 15 to 25 objects, one at a time. When the last one has been around the circle, the items are hidden. Players remove their blindfolds and write lists of what passed.

HAND SHADOWS

A source of light such as a candle lantern or flashlight, a small tent wall area, and a pair of agile hands are all you need for the endless fun of hand shadows. This pastime has delighted people for ages, being simple in concept yet creative and thoroughly challenging. It seems custom-made for long winter evenings in a tent, where walls form the perfect screen on which to project the figures your hands conjure up.

To get you started, here are several figures to try. Add motion when you can by making wings flap, ears wiggle, and mouths talk. Two friends can stage a conversation or whole play, making their shadow creatures interact. There are no doubt fantastically intricate shadows waiting to be created by three or four tentfellows working together, using good signals, steady hands, and infinite patience. Light the lantern and gear up for an evening of pleasant sport!

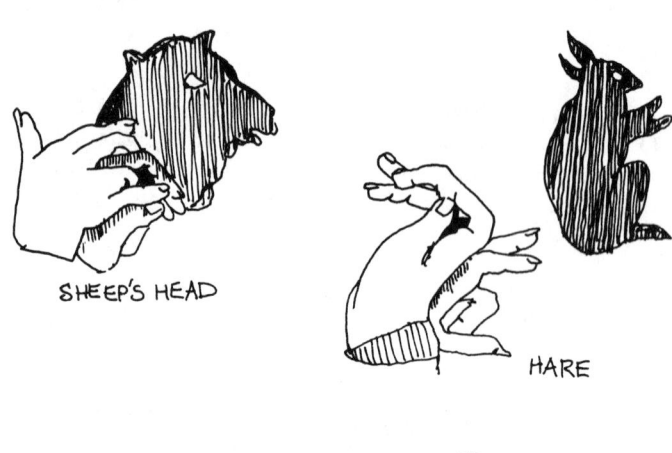

SHEEP'S HEAD

HARE

ELEPHANT

SWAN

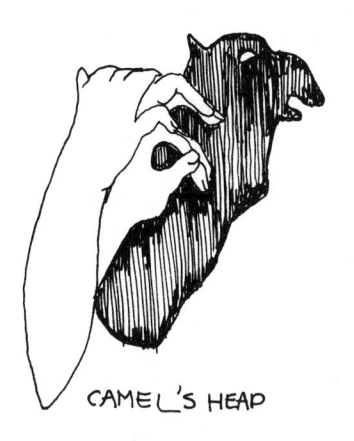

CAMEL'S HEAD

BIRD IN FLIGHT

GOAT

EAGLE

SHAKESPEARE

BULL'S HEAD

MAKE SOME MUSIC

In addition to using your voice in the usual ways (solo, duet, group, rounds, answering songs), there are many other ways to make music in the wilds. Try your hand at some of the **instruments** described in the Make-at-Home section of this book (mouthbow, wood harmonica, one-string dulcimer) and see the Catalog section for ideas about the multitude of totable instruments available in music stores: harmonica, jew's harp, bamboo flute, ocarina, pan pipes, and more.

And have you ever **played your nose**? Hold your left index finger snug against your left nostril, closing it off. While humming through your nose, make twanging strokes against your right nostril with your right index finger. Hawaiian tunes and oldies such as ''Poor Butterfly'' and ''I'm Forever Blowing Bubbles'' seem just made for this mode of musical expression.

Then there's **Name That Tune**: One person slaps out the rhythm of a mystery tune on his leg and the others try to guess what it is. The successful guesser than takes a turn trying to stump the crowd with his own choice.

Dueling harmonicas can go on for hours, answering each other's challenging musical phrase.

Spoons. If you don't travel with two spoons, borrow one from a trailmate and whomp up some good rhythm with the pair. The clickety-clack of well-wielded spoons adds real zip to downhome ditties.

To play: Put the handle of one spoon between the index and middle fingers of one hand and the handle of the other between the middle and ring fingers of the same hand. The rounded bottoms of the spoons should face each other and the handles be tucked into the palm of your hand. Hold the spoons loose enough so the bottoms are slightly apart but the spoons still aligned, and beat out a steady rhythm in the palm of your other hand. Try beating the spoons on your knee, and between your thigh and the other hand held palm downward about eight inches above your thigh. Or hold your hand with the palm facing sideways so the spoon edges touch it in rapid succession.

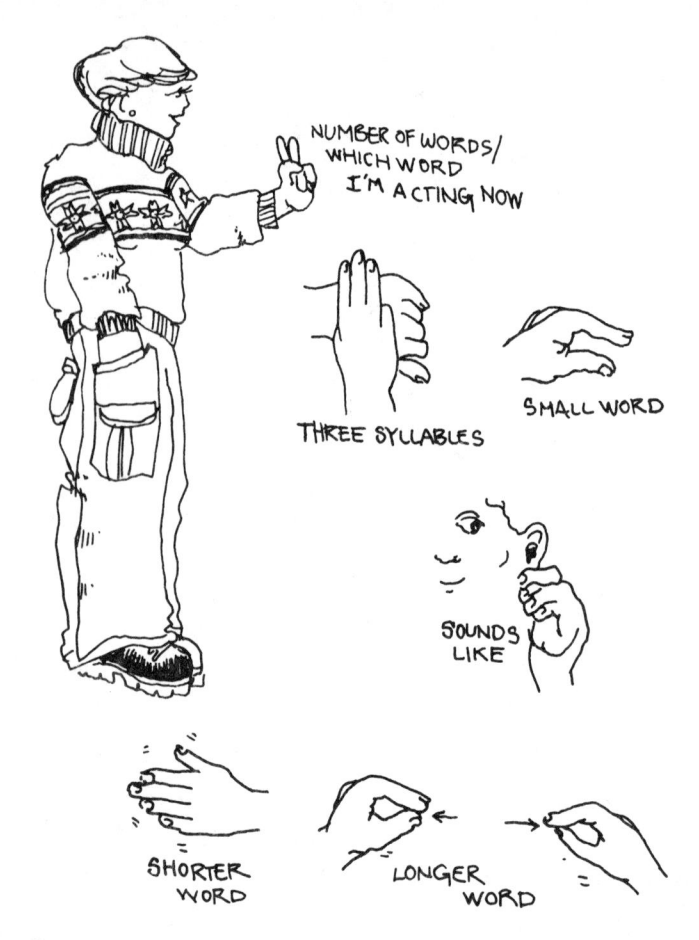

WILDERNESS CHARADES

Adapt the familiar games of Charades to a wilderness setting by acting out the names of flowers, birds or mammals. Here are some that would be a fair challenge:

Flowers: St. John's Wort, false Solomon's seal, wild ginger, cow parsnip, dirty socks, youth-on-age

Birds: great horned owl, American goldfinch, cedar waxwing, yellow-bellied sapsucker, least sandpiper, cinnamon teal

Mammals: porcupine, pocket gopher, bushy-tailed woodrat, bobcat, snowshoe hare, river otter

Remember the basic signals used by the person pantomiming a word or phrase.

DETECTIVE

One person puts a large number of objects together and covers them up. Include natural things as well as items from packs. Have everyone gather around and remove the cover for two minutes. Then cover the cache again and have all players write a list of what they saw. The person with the longest list wins a trenchcoat and cigar!

TIE ONE ON . . . KNOT GAMES

All hikers can benefit from knowing a few basic knots and their uses, but many of us either don't take the time to learn knots in the first place or let our skills slip for lack of practice. Get out your nylon line or extra boot laces and spend some time in camp tying these five useful knots. Practice all five for 15 minutes, then put aside all samples and drawings and try tying them with no assists.

For each knot you do correctly, collect one edible goody from each trailmate (if he's out of snacks, get him to promise you a beer or a milkshake on the drive home). If any adroit camper gets all five right, he should receive a *big* treat from the group — breakfast in bed, his tent set up for him, a luxurious massage, or part of his load carried next day.

A **Square Knot** ties together two pieces of rope.

A **Slip Knot** makes a loop which can be changed after the knot is tied.

A **Bowline** is used to make a loop whose size remains fixed after it's tied.

A **Tautline Hitch** forms a loop that stays the same size under tension but can be loosened to adjust.

A **Clove Hitch** is a nonslip way to lash objects together, tie rope to a tree, etc.

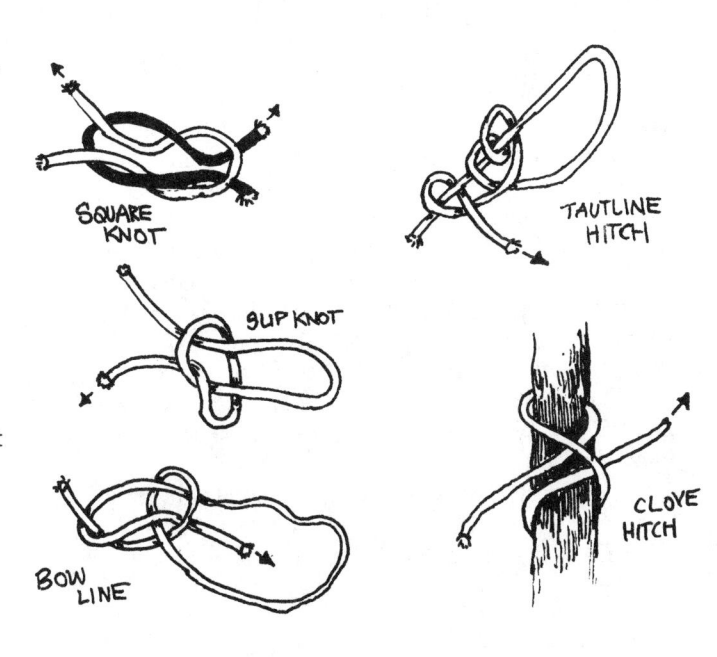

89

STRING FIGURES

What wonders can be wrought with a simple loop of string manipulated by your fingers! Perhaps you remember making Cat's Cradle or Jacob's Ladder as a child. Well, a backpack trip is the perfect setting for renewing and expanding your skill with string figures. The equipment is weightless, the challenge ample for the keenest mind, and successful coordination between brain and hands distinctly satisfying.

This form of amusement is ancient and virtually universal, practiced all over the world by both children and adults. At times it reaches elaborate complexity. String figures were often formed as visual accompaniments to storytelling among primitive peoples. They can be woven by one person alone using hands, sometimes assisted by feet and even teeth. Two people can cooperate on a pattern that requires four hands, or they can work a figure by using the left hand of one and the right hand of the other, while their other hands make yet another pattern. Figures can show action by having built-in movable parts.

Use a length of string about six feet long (eight wraps around your loose fist is a good measure), tied into a loop. The hank of line you probably carry in your pack will work fine if you didn't bring along a piece of string from home.

Before launching into a few figures, let's define some terms used frequently in the instructions.

The **fingers** are called thumb, index, middle, ring and little.

Usual position of the hands is with palms facing each other and fingers pointed up.

Openings may vary, but probably half the recorded figures begin with the same one, the traditional Cat's Cradle. The object of the opening is to arrange the big string loop on your hands so that a number of secondary loops cross from the fingers of one hand to the fingers of the other, stretched between the hands held in their usual position.

Loop names: The loops are named for the fingers on which they're placed, such as right index loop, left little finger loop. Every finger loop has two strings and usually these pass between the hands to form the strings of finger loops on the opposite hand.

String names: The strings of the finger loops which leave the finger from the side nearest you are *near strings*; the strings which leave the finger from the side farthest from you are *far strings*. If a finger has two loops on it, they're called *upper* and *lower loops*, each with near and far strings. A string crossing the palm is a *palmar string*.

The final object, the pattern, is formed by manipulating the strings which were put on the fingers in the opening. There are many possible movements, some quite complex.

A good starting figure is the **Fishing Spear**, which begins with the loop hooked behind the thumb and little finger of each hand passing across the palms.

1. Pick up the left palmar string from underneath with your right index finger, twisting the loop several times by rotating your index finger as you pull your hands apart.

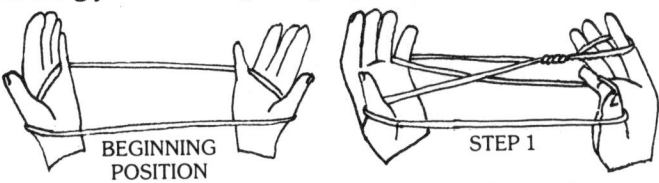

BEGINNING POSITION

STEP 1

2. With your left index finger pick up from below the string crossing your right palm, being sure to pick it up between the strings of the right index loop.

3. Pull your hands apart, releasing your right thumb and little finger. The handle of the spear is held on the right index finger and the points on the left thumb, index and little finger.

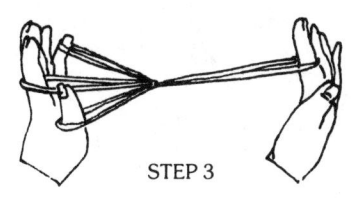

STEP 3

Cat's Whiskers is a slightly more complex figure. It is especially fun because it is also the basis from which the Jacob's Ladder pattern evolves, and a final quick assist by a friend produces Farmer's Pants!

1. Put the loop behind the thumb, across the palm and behind the little finger of each hand. Spread your hands apart.

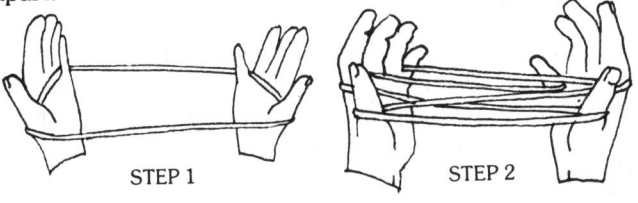

STEP 1

STEP 2

2. Put your right index finger under the left palmar string and spread your hands, pulling the string back. Repeat with the other hand. You have formed the cat's cradle, the most common opening for string figures.

3. Release the string from both thumbs. Reach under with both thumbs and pick up the far little finger string on the backs of the thumbs, then return the thumbs to their original position.

4. Put your thumbs over the near index strings and pick up the far index strings on the backs of the thumbs.

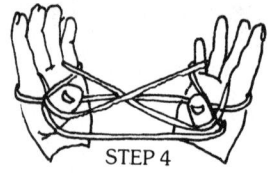

STEP 4

5. Release the little fingers. Put the little fingers over the string nearest them and pick up the next string on the backs of the little fingers, returning them to their original position.

6. Release the thumbs. You have Cat's Whiskers, which, of course, look best hooked under your nose!

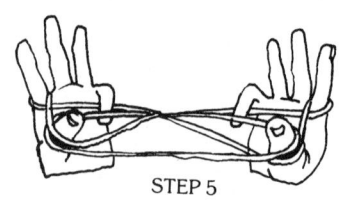

STEP 5

STEP 6

Jacob's Ladder is formed by taking Cat's Whiskers just a few steps farther.

7. Put the thumbs over both index strings and pick up the near little finger string on the backs of the thumbs, returning them to position.

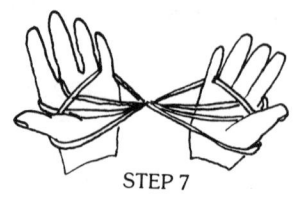

STEP 7

8. With the right thumb and index finger pick up the left near index string and place it over the left thumb.

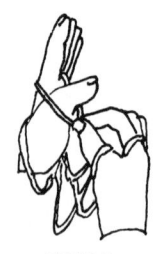

STEP 8

9. With the right thumb and index finger lift the lower left near thumb string over the string just transferred and drop it. Repeat for the other hand.

10. Insert each index finger from above into the small triangle formed by the palmar string twisting around the

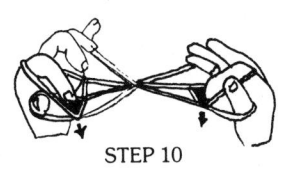

STEP 10

thumb loop. Turning the palms down, release the string from the little fingers, spread your fingers and separate your hands to tighten the strings. Jacob's Ladder will appear!

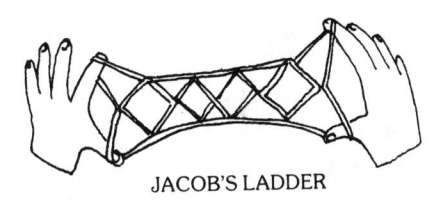

JACOB'S LADDER

Now while you hold Jacob's Ladder in place, have a friend create **Farmer's Pants** by gently pulling the bottom string downward with his index fingers from the two points on either side of the middle bottom triangle while you release your thumbs.

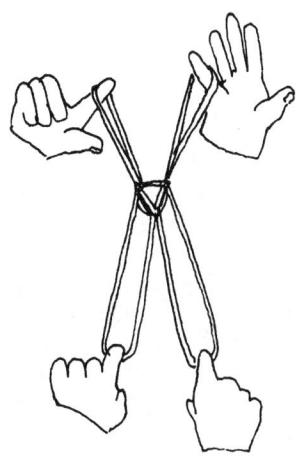

FARMER'S PANTS

93

PUZZLE ANSWERS (for puzzles on pages 76-77)

1. 8 have three sides painted, 12 have two sides painted, and 6 have one side painted.

2. 13 dimes and 7 quarters.

3.

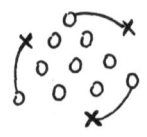

4. Marco was always in the boat. The first trip across, he took the rabbit, returning with nothing. On the second trip he took the cabbage, returning with the rabbit. On the third trip he took the fox, returning with nothing. On the fourth trip he took the rabbit.

5. The number 5.

6.

2	9	4
7	5	3
6	1	8

7. Facetious and abstemious.

8. 39 minutes.

9.

10.

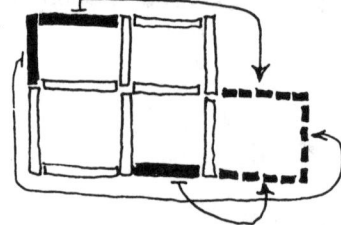

11.

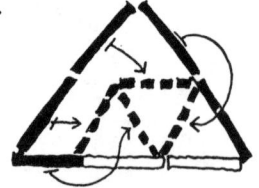

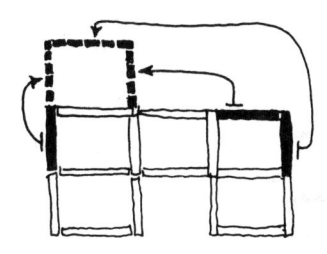

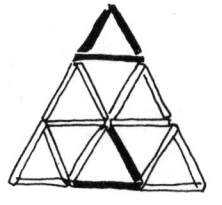

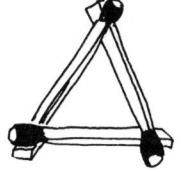

12.

13.

14.

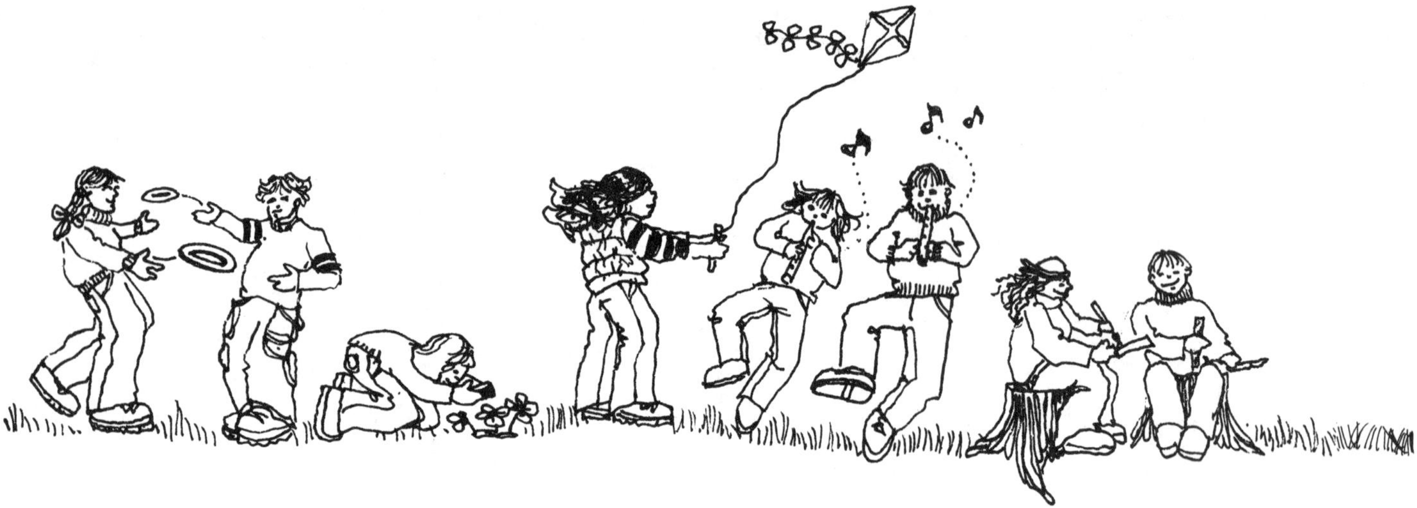

Section III:
CATALOG OF PACKABLE PLEASURES

Here is a far-ranging survey of interesting items a backpacker can buy and take along for his pleasure on the trail. Many things are generally available at certain types of retail stores; those will be listed first. Others can be found at both retail and mail-order outlets, and I'll list sources I know about. A few books that can enhance your wilderness experience are presented, along with mail-order sources for some of them. You'll find a **complete address for suppliers at the end of the section.**

Approximate prices are given, but these vary among sources and are constantly changing. My suggestion, if you want to order something by mail, is to request a current catalog from the supplier. It will also outline postage and handling costs, which differ among suppliers.

TOY STORES
DEPARTMENT STORES
STATIONERY STORES

A wealth of toys suitable for trail use can be found in toy stores and departments. It would be impossible to list all the hundreds of individual games on the market now, but we'll describe enough examples so that you can glimpse the possibilities. Take a leisurely tour through the toy outlets in your town before your next hike; choose items that please you or get ideas for adaptations you can make yourself. Look at toys and games with an eye to how they might be stripped down to only their truly essential elements for backpacking use. For instance, there are dozens of word games built on the cup/dice/timer principle. When you take one of these in your pack, all you really need are the rules and dice. Heavy parts of many games can be replaced with candies from your pack, stones, cones, or other objects in the wilds (see complete list at front of this book).

Travel versions of many **old favorites** can be found, scaled down in size and weight and frequently magnetized or adapted in some other way to motion and unstable playing surfaces. Look for checkers, chess, backgammon and cribbage, all from $2 up. A tiny deck of playing cards costs under $1. A travel edition of Scrabble is fairly heavy but might appeal to a group of dedicated players ($14). An 8-inch-square Chinese checker game can be found for $8. An erasable magic slate (under $1) saves paper for such games as tic tac toe and hangman.

Wooden and plastic **pocket games** abound for one or more players, covering a vast range from peg solitaire to tic tac toe to soccer, and priced from $1.50 to $7. Pocket puzzles are available as transparent plastic cubes with mazes and balls inside, three-dimensional interlocking blocks and wires, number puzzles set in frames, crossword puzzles, mazes, and wooden dice puzzles to reassemble in various combinations. There are modern copies of the time-honored yoke puzzle, tangram, and lovers' knot.

A whole family of **paper and pencil games** in tablet form can be found for $1.50 each: crosswords, mazes, dot games, brain teasers, coded puzzles and fill-in stories.

Word games such as Boggle, Perquacky, Ad-Lib and Spill & Spell are natural lightweight travelers. They begin at around $3.50; the more elaborate versions may cost as much as $8. All are challenging enough to provide amusement for a good long stretch of tent confinement.

Card games requiring special decks start at $3. You'll find old favorites from your childhood days such as Pit, Flinch, and Rook, along with an extensive array of newer card games, simple to complex. Tarot cards used in fortune telling are available for $7 and more.

Various **action toys** line the shelves: yo-yos (from 60 cents), paddle balls (50 cents), plastic and wooden boomerangs costing from $1.80, frisbees (simple to fancy from $1.35 to $6) and whiz rings (39 cents each . . . juggle three or keep two in flight with a friend), all kinds of kites from $1 to $13 (choose the kites whose struts are removable; soft kites made of fabric which can be rolled up are most totable and lasting). One special kind of kaleidoscope is a delight for wilderness use; it contains only angled mirrors which produce fascinating patterns when trees, clouds, water and other natural elements are viewed through it.

Some toy stores carry a selection of small **telescopes** and hand **magnifying lenses** which can be used to study the heavens and the many intriguing tiny things found in the wilds. A 30-power telescope can be purchased for around $13, a 40-power telescope with tripod for $23. Hand lenses come with one, two, or three interchangeable lenses in varying degrees of magnification and range from $1 to $19.

Occasionally toy stores have a music department with simple **instruments** ranging from 60-cent kazoos to $7 wooden recorders. In between you may find a wooden harmonica (95 cents), hand drum ($1.30), sand blocks ($2.75), handle castanets ($2.75), rhythm sticks ($1.25), wood sounders and blocks with mallets ($1 to $3.50).

ART SUPPLY OUTLETS

Lightweight and compact forms of **artistic tools** are many and varied. A tiny metal box of six water colors and a short brush costs 60 cents; larger water color sets start at $1.50 and are as simple or elaborate as you wish. Pastels in sets begin at less than $1, charcoals at $3, felt pens at $1, and acrylic paints at $5 for five tubes. Sketch pads can be small (4 by 7 inches) or enormous and can be had for 75 cents up to a few dollars.

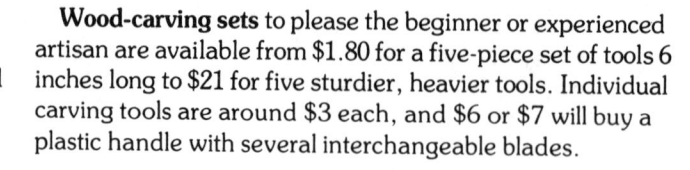

Wood-carving sets to please the beginner or experienced artisan are available from $1.80 for a five-piece set of tools 6 inches long to $21 for five sturdier, heavier tools. Individual carving tools are around $3 each, and $6 or $7 will buy a plastic handle with several interchangeable blades.

Origami sets of colored papers to fold into designs come in many sizes, including a packet of 60 4-inch multicolored squares with patterns for less than $1.

MUSIC STORES

Music stores vary considerably in the number of simple and folk instruments they carry, so you'd be wise to scout around by telephone if your town has several.

For less than $1 you can find several varieties and shapes of humazoos, kazoos, and even a nose flute! Harmonicas grow from the 1½-inch 8-note model ($2.50) to a long chromatic one with a $100 price tag, but the most popular sizes cost $6 or $7, are available in several keys and fit nicely in your pocket. Other **instruments to blow** are: ocarinas (or sweet potatoes) from $3.50 to $5, pan pipes from $5 to $26, slide whistles and plastic transverse flutes for $4 and up, recorders in many voices (plastic ones cost $5 and up, wooden ones $8 and up), penny whistles in a wide range from $2.50 to $20 (these are six-hole flutes with straight up-and-down fingering, a two-octave range, available in different keys, made of brass, tin and wood, and also called flageolets). Bamboo transverse flutes are challenging to learn and larger than most hikers would want to carry, but their soft, haunting tones fit in beautifully with the outdoors. These flutes are 20 to 24 inches long and cost $12 to $20.

NOSE FLUTE

OCARINA

PAN PIPES

A delightful parade of **rhythm instruments** can be discovered in your favorite music store, with something for everyone's wallet and skill level. The funkiest are musical spoons and rhythm "bones" ($3.50 a set). Claves, wood blocks, hand drums, castanets and finger cymbals can all be purchased for $2 or $3. The most exotic percussion instrument we encountered in our survey was a wooden kirikiko from Japan for $14. It consists of two handles at the ends of an arch made by thin wooden pieces strung together at one end. The player manipulates this fluid arch to create clacking sounds as the wood slats bump against each other in domino fashion. It is said that an expert can get two rhythms going at once!

Wooden **drum boxes** come in several sizes and prices, mostly bulkier than backpackers would like, but for $8 you can get one that measures 3 by 7 inches. Its tone, when struck with a mallet, is gentle and pleasing. Striking the box in different places produces varying sounds because of slotted patterns in the wood.

Another instrument of African origin is the **kalimba** (or thumb piano), a resonating gourd or wooden box with metal reeds mounted on the top, played with the thumbs. The highest pitched, celeste, is smallest and costs around $19. Lower-voiced, larger kalimbas are a few dollars more. Or make one from a kit (see below) and save. Care must be taken in packing your kalimba because the pitch of the reeds will change if they are moved in the bridge. But you may become so enamored of this instrument's soft tones that you'll make a place for it in your pack, possibly wrapped in an extra shirt for safety.

A fun drone instrument for accompanying singing or other melodies is the **jew's harp**, available for $1.50 to $3. It is a rigid metal keyhole-shaped piece held against the mouth, with a flexible metal spring that is twanged by a finger. Your open mouth provides a resonating chamber. The **limber jack** (or jane) could be called a rhythm instrument, and you may find a kit to make a small one for $2.25. This wooden jointed figure is held on a stick above a flexible board. When either the figure or the board moves, the limber jack dances and taps out a rhythm.

MUSIC BY MAIL

The following musical instruments are available by mail from the sources listed (addresses on pages 108-9)

Bamboo flute: Guitar's Friend; John Niemi

Mouth bow: Alpine Dulcimer Company (listed by them as the Arkansas picking bow); Guitar's Friend

Limber jack kit: Hughes Dulcimer Company, Country Ways

Recorder, pennywhistle, drum box, jew's harp, spoons, bones, kalimba, kazoo, nose flute, etc.: Guitar's Friend

Kalimba kit (thumb piano): Country Ways; Guitar's Friend

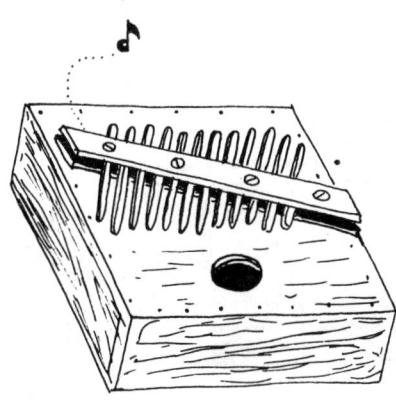

KALIMBA

MAIL-ORDER GAMES

Constellation [Star Game] by Vinson Brown, about $3: available at some book stores or from Naturegraph Publishers, Inc. To aid you in learning the stars, this set of cards shows 36 constellations, telling when and where they can be found, and the relative brilliance of the stars in them. Some group games are suggested, but a lone traveler could also enjoy this set.

Competitive Compass Game, Beginner's Compass Game, from Silva Company, 75 cents and $1. Cards with instructions for group games which give practice in following bearings.

The Pollination Game, $5.95 from The Nature Company. Color card deck with information about plant growth and the ecological systems that support it, leading to a variety of games.

The Predator Game, $4.50 from The Nature Company. Animals replace the numbers on traditional cards according to their place in the natural food chain of a forest.

Traveling cribbage, chess/checkers, backgammon, about $3 each from Eastern Mountain Sports.

Tangram Kit, $1.75 from Dover Publications. Two sets of tangram pieces on cardboard, plus 120 tangrams with solutions.

Addresses of suppliers on pages 108-109.

KITES

Most kite suppliers have a few soft, foldable offerings in their catalogs. Mini-foils and para-foils have no sticks and fold up to pocket size. Other styles have removable struts or fold up for packing, and come in a dizzying array of shapes. Prices range from about $8 for a cloth delta style or Chinese bird kite, to $15 for a mini-foil made from nylon spinnaker cloth, to a $40 eagle with a wingspan of more than five feet.

These folks will send you an enticing catalog to browse through (addresses on pages 108-9):
  Come Fly a Kite
  Go Fly a Kite
  The Kite Factory
  The Kite Shop
  Kyte Kingdom
  Nantucket Kiteman 'N' Kitelady
  Mini-foil and para-foil kites are also available from Pacific Search Press, and Chinese bird kites from Early Winters.

Another flying item is the **boomerang** and in addition to retail outlets, you can buy boomerangs from:
  The Boomerang Man. His brochure lists dozens of styles and sizes, with suggestions to help you choose the right one.

TWO NIFTY NATURE ITEMS

Audubon bird call, about $3.50, at local Audubon Societies or by mail from Audubon Workshop (address on page 108) When you twist the handle, the resin-covered pewter plug rubs against wood to make sounds which attract birds.

Sunprint Kit, $3.50 from The Nature Company (address on page 109). Makes prints from leaves and other objects on light-sensitive paper in the sun.

Addresses of suppliers on pages 108-109.

BOOKS

Mail order suppliers are listed for some, but you can also track down a book at your local library, order it directly from the publisher (addresses in *Books in Print* in library or bookstore), or have your favorite bookstore order it for you (there's no charge for this service).

Be Expert with Map and Compass, Bjorn Kjellstrom, Charles Scribner's Sons, New York 1976. A do-it-yourself course with exercises for practicing newfound skills. $6.95. Order from Eastern Mountain Sports, Recreational Equipment, Inc., or The Ski Hut.

Edible Plants Card Deck, Calvin P. Burt and Frank G. Heyl, available in eastern U.S. and western U.S. versions. Pocket-sized plant identification cards with color photographs and detailed descriptions of the most important edible and poisonous plants. About $6. From The Nature Company.

A Field Guide to Animal Tracks, Olaus Murie, Houghton Mifflin Company, Boston 1975 (part of the Peterson Field Guide series). More than just an aid to identifying tracks and droppings, this book is full of fascinating animal, bird, and insect lore. $4.95.

Knowing the Outdoors in the Dark, Vinson Brown, Collier Books, New York 1972. Especially helpful in putting you at ease in the night world, learning how to listen to, observe and appreciate it. $2.95.

The New Games Book, edited by Andrew Fleugelman, Doubleday, Garden City, New York. Friendly, gentle and spirited ways to play so that everyone has a good time. $4.95. From Mother's Bookshelf.

The Sager Weathercaster, Raymond M. Sager, Weather Publications, Pleasantville, NY 1969. Use with a pocket altimeter to predict local weather for the next 24 hours. About $9. From L.L. Bean and Eastern Mountain Sports.

The Stars, A New Way to See Them, H.A. Rey, Houghton Mifflin Company, Boston 1976. Basic, clear information about the worlds above us. $5.95.

String Figures and How to Make Them, Caroline Furness Jayne, Dover Publications, Inc., New York 1962. First published in 1906, this is the most scholarly and complete work on string figures you'll find. $3.50. From Mother's Bookshelf or Dover Publications.

Whitney's Star Finder, Charles A. Whitney, Alfred A. Knopf, New York 1977. Explanations of many celestial activities, aids to identifying stars and planets, using the sky as a clock, and more. $5.95.

ITEMS FOR VIEWING TINY OR FARAWAY OBJECTS
(addresses on pages 108-109)

Pocket microscopes weigh just a few ounces, are three or four inches long, and cost from $6 to $60, depending on magnifying power and optical quality. From Waters, Inc., Edmund Scientific Company, and The Nature Company.

Illuminated **pocket magnifiers** are found for about $16 from The Nature Company (ten-power, 6 inches long) and Eastern Mountain Sports (five- or ten-power).

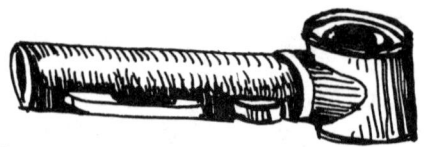

A dual-purpose **pocket micro-telescope** is available for about $13 from Edmund Scientific Company.

A **pocket telescope** (4 ounces, 3½ inches long) can be had for approximately $30 from The Nature Company.

Larger telescopes that are still within the carrying range of some hikers can be found at Waters, Inc. for $20 (ten-power, 9 ounces, 10¼ inches long), Edmund Scientific Company for $30 (ten-power, 11 ounces, 10 inches long) or about $70 (13X to 40X zoom, with tripod, 2 pounds, 12 ounces).

You can even get **a kit** to build your own eight-power telescope that is 18 inches long (about $9 from Edmund Scientific Company).

Hand lenses (also called pocket magnifiers) can be obtained from several mail order suppliers in a variety of prices. Round lenses fold into a plastic housing; most weigh half an ounce or less. Doublet and triplet lenses are cemented together, rather than being separate lenses that can be used independently. A single five-power lens may cost around $4.50 (Eastern Mountain Sports), a double five-power student's model $.85, a doublet eight-power lens $5 and a triplet ten or fourteen-power lens $23 (The Nature Company). Another ten-power triplet lens is found at Edmund Scientific Company for about $19. This outlet also carries several other folding pocket magnifiers from $1.75 to $7. A variable magnifier with three separate lenses gives magnifications of 5X, 10X and 20X for $8 (Eastern Mountain Sports).

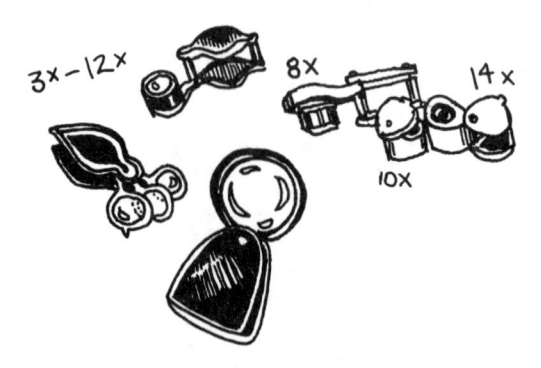

106

Magnifier boxes are one-inch cubes of lucite with removable four-power magnifier tops, for storing small flower buds or anything else you want to keep and examine at close range. A dozen weigh 4 ounces and cost $4.20 at The Nature Company.

Fixed focus magnifiers have a lens focused at the end of a lucite enclosure, permitting observation of live specimens, plants and so forth. A detachable transparent base incorporates a 20mm measuring scale. The 8X magnifier costs around $5 and the 4X wide-field magnifier $7 (from The Nature Company). Both are palm-sized.

Addresses of suppliers on pages 108-109.

SUPPLIERS

Here are the full addresses of mail-order suppliers. Request a catalog giving current prices and mail-order instructions.

Alpine Dulcimer Company, Box 566, Boulder, CO 80306

Audubon Workshop, 1501 Paddock Drive, Northbrook, IL 60062

Boomerang Man, 311 Park Avenue, Monroe, LA 71201

Come Fly a Kite, 900 North Point, Ghirardelli Square, San Francisco, CA 94109

Country Ways, Incorporated, 3500 Highway 101 South, Minnetonka, MN 55343

Dover Publications, Inc., 180 Varick St., New York, NY 10014

Early Winters, Ltd., 110 Prefontaine Place South, Seattle, WA 98104

Eastern Mountain Sports, Vose Farm Road, Peterborough, NH 03458

Edmund Scientific Corporation, Edscorp Building, Barrington, NJ 08007

Go Fly a Kite, Box AA, East Haddam, CT 06423

Guitar's Friend, Route 1, Box 200, Sandpoint, ID 83864

Hughes Dulcimer Company, 8665 W. 13th Avenue, Denver, CO 80215

The Kite Factory, Box 9081, Seattle, WA 98109

The Kite Shop, 542 St. Peter Street, New Orleans, LA 70116

Kyte Kingdom, P.O. Box 3371, Boulder, CO 80307

L.L. Bean, Freeport, ME 04032

Mother's Bookshelf, P.O. Box 70, Hendersonville, NC 28739

Nantucket Kiteman 'N' Kitelady, Box 1356, Nantucket, MA 02554

The Nature Company, P.O. Box 7137, Berkeley, CA 94707

Naturegraph Publishers, Inc., Healdsburg, CA 95448

John Niemi, Box 1517, Eugene, OR 97440

Pacific Search Press, 715 Harrison Street, Seattle, WA 98109

Recreational Equipment, Inc., P.O. Box C-88125, Seattle, WA 98140

Silva Company, 2466 North State Road 39, LaPorte, IN 46350

The Ski Hut, P.O. Box 309, Berkeley, CA 94701

Waters, Inc., 111 E. Sheridan Street, Ely, MN 55731

Index

A

Albanian Dwarfs, 78
Art equipment, 100
Audubon bird call, 49, 104

B

Backgammon, 98, 103
Bird calling, 49
Block puzzle, *make-at-home*, 20
Blow bubbles, 81
Body and senses games, 81-93
Boil This Down, 67
Bolo, mountain, *make-at-home*, 30
Boomerang, *make-at-home*, 24
   mail-order, 104
Botanical dictionary, 58, 59-61
Bubbles, blowing, 81
Buttonholer puzzle, *make-at-home*, 22
Buzz saw, *make-at-home*, 29

C

Card games, 78-80
Cartographer's Delight, 64
Cat's Whiskers, 91
Charades, wilderness, 88
Checkers, 98, 103
Chess, 98, 103
Chinese checkers, 98
Cinquain, 49
Collages and wall hangings,
   from collected materials, 82
Collecting,
   feathers, 47
   scats, 47
Compass
   finding your way back, 54-55
   orienting, 53
   parts of, 53
   reaching landmark, 54
   taking bearing, 53
Compass games, 103
Constellation game, the, 103
Contour puzzle, *make-at-home*, 21
Cribbage, 98, 103
Cross flute, *make-at-home*, 38
Cup and Ball, *make-at-home*, 29

D

Dara, game board, 56
   how to play, 75
Daylight, how much left, ways to calculate, 51
Detective, 88
Dice, Two-Sided, 72
Dictionary, botanical, 58, 59-61
Dulcimer, one-string, 86
   make-at-home, 36

E

Endless Chain, 62
Evening wildlife observation, 46
Expansion, 70

F

Farmer's Pants, 91
Feather collecting, 47
Finger cymbals, *make-at-home*, 38
Finger puzzles, 76-77
   answers, 94
Fishing Spear, 91
Flora and fauna, identification games, 49
Flute, bamboo, 86
Fox and Geese, *make-at-home*, 33
Frame-making idea, 82

G

Game board, *make-at-home*, 32

Game boards, 56-57
Grass blowing, 81
Granny's Backpack, 63

H

Haiku, 49
Hand shadows, 84
Harmonica, 86
    Dueling Harmonicas, 86
    wood, *make-at-home*, 36
Harmonica, wood, *make-at-home*, 36
Harp, matchbox, *make-at-home*, 39
Hexer puzzle, *make-at-home*, 23
Hig-Pig, 65

I

I'm Thinking Of . . . , 67
Identification games, flora and fauna, 45, 49

J

Jacob's Ladder, 92
Jew's harp, 86
Juggling, 81

K

Kazoo, comb-and-paper, *make-at-home*, 40
Keep Your Eyes Peeled, 69
Kite flying, 82

sources, 104
Knots, games for learning, 89

L

Landmarks
    how to reach, 54
    finding your way back, 54-55
Lists galore, 67

M

Magic Fifteen, 76
Map skills, 52
Magnifiers, sources, 106
Match games, 73
Microscopes, sources, 106
Migration game, *make-at-home*, 33
Mountain bolo, *make-at-home*, 30
Mouthbow, 86
    make-at-home version, 40
Musical instruments, sources, 86

N

Nail puzzle, *make-at-home*, 19
Name games, flora and fauna
    scientific names, 58
Name Stretch, 62
Name That Tune, 86
Nature survey, intensive, 47

Nine Men's Morris, game board, 57
    how to play, 75

O

Ocarina, 86
One Minute of Words, 70
Ooooh-Aaaah, 83
Orchestra, instant, *make-at-home*, 39-40
Orientation, with compass, 53
Orientation, without compass, 51
Origami, 100

P

Paddle and Ball, *make-at-home*, 26
Pin and Balls, *make-at-home*, 27
    ring version, 28
Paddle Golf, *make-at-home*, 27
Pan pipes, 86
Pitch pennies, 81
Plant press, *make-at-home*, 34
Plaster casts of animal tracks, 47
Playing pieces, suggestions for, *xiii*
Playing Your Nose, 86
Poems
    haiku, 49
    cinquain, 49
Points for Pairs, 69
Pollination Game, the, 103
Predator Game, the, 103

111

Profiles, 70
Put and Take, *make-at-home*, 32

Q

Quick Change, 70

R

Ring version of Pin and Balls, *make-at-home*, 28
Rock game, 46

S

Sandwich Game, game board, 56
    how to play, 74
Scat collecting, 46
Scavenger hunt, nature, 46
Scientific name games, 58
Scrabble, 98
Sensory games, 83
Sentenced, 64
Sing Out, 63
Six-sided Stumpers, *make-at-home*, 31
Sketches, animal tracks, 48
Sleeping Giant, 81
Smell and Tell, 83
Solitaire, *make-at-home*, 33

Speed, 79
Spoons
    a card game, 78
    a musical instrument, 87
Stargazing, 50
Stick puzzles, 77
Story Ball, 72
Strawhorn, *make-at-home*, 39
String and Bead puzzle, *make-at-home*, 18
String figures, 90-93
Sun calculations
    position, 50
    daylight time, how much left, 51
Sun print kit, 104

T

Tangram, *make-at-home*, 24
    mail-order kit, 103
Teamwork Tales, 72
Telescopes, sources, 106
Tic Tac Toe, number 71
Tie one on, 89
Touching Test, 83
Tongue Tanglers, 65
Tracks, animal,
    casts of, 47
    sketches of, 48

Triangle Capture, 71
Twenty Questions, 62
Twitch, 80
Two-Sided Dice, 72

V

Volga Boatman, 76

W

Wall hangings and collages, 82
Waterscope, 48
    make-at-home, 35
Watt Zynonym?, 64
Weave-a-Word, 71
Weaving, using collected materials, 83
What Am I?, 66
Whimsical Word Weaving, 72
Whittling, 81
Wilderness Charades, 88
Wildlife observation, at night, 46
Woodcarving, 81
    tools for, 100
Word Derivation, 70
Word Grid, 68
Word Pairs, 62
Word Weaving, whimsical, 72